BBC CHILDREN'S BOOKS
Published by the Penguin Group
Penguin Books Ltd, 80 Strand, London WC2R 0RL, England
Published by BBC Children's Character Books, 2009
10 9 8 7 6 5 4 3 2 1
Text and design © BBC Children's Character Books, 2009
Newsround © BBC 2009
All rights reserved.
www.bbc.co.uk/cbbc
ISBN 13: 978 1 405 90600 5
Printed in China

Thanks to the following press packers:
Josh Braddock p7; Joe Tosh p17; Alex Milne p19; Rhema Howell-Smith p38; Rose Linton p41; Diana Savchuk p47;
Jake Schepuck p69; Hannah Snee p78; Caitlin Dempster p91.

Written by Mandy Archer and Stephanie Clarkson

newsround

Yearbook
Your news, your stories

Contents

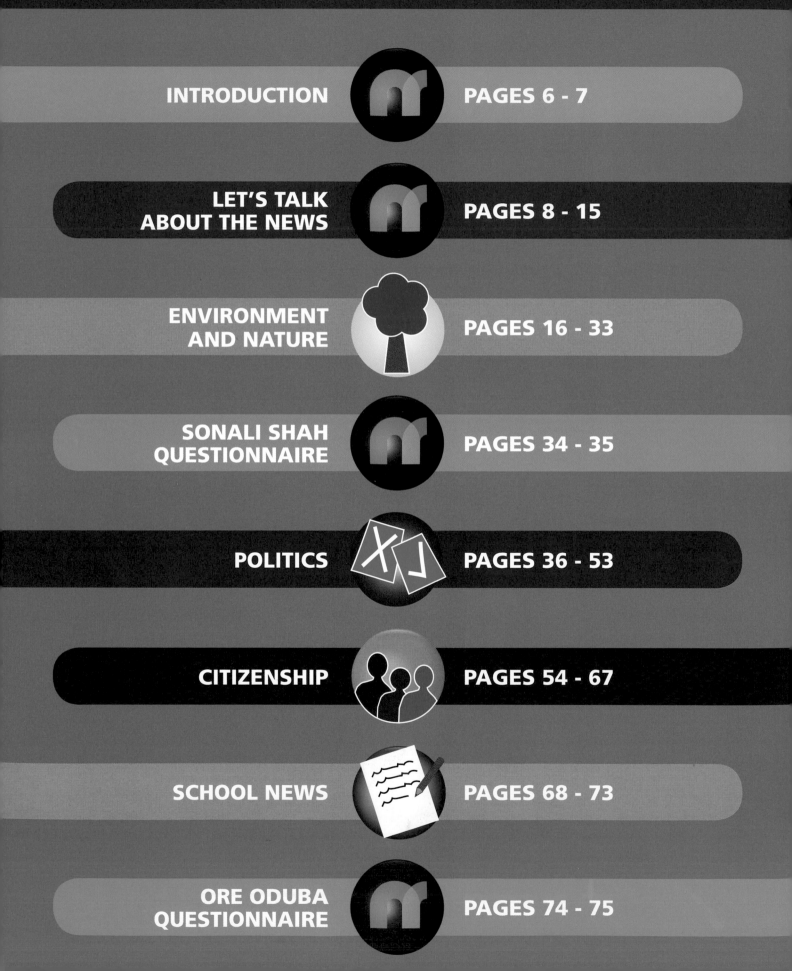

Newsround, old and new

John Craven presenting Newsround in the 1970s, and Ore Oduba presenting Newsround today.

When Newsround first started back in 1972 it was only supposed to be on television for six weeks. BBC bosses weren't sure that children would be interested in the news but there was a gap in the TV schedules so they decided to give it a go. A handful of staff were given a few typewriters and a corner of the main BBC newsroom. To say the experiment worked is probably an understatement! Thirty-seven years on, Newsround now has 36 programmes every week. It's on BBC One, BBC Two and the CBBC channel and it has one of the most frequently updated kids' websites in the UK.

So what's the secret to Newsround's success?

Well, we think it's because we always listen to you! We get hundreds of emails from children across the UK every week, we visit schools regularly and we constantly ask our viewers to tell us what they think about our content. Many of the stories we cover have been suggested by kids who watch our shows or who visit our website. Listening to what you have to say is really important to us - if we didn't pay attention, Newsround might not have made it this far!

Sinéad Rocks
Newsround and Sportsround Production Editor

YOUR NEWS, YOUR STORIES...

Newsround really is all about the kind of news that you want to hear about. That's why it is so important to get your opinions and stories on the events happening around you, be it locally or globally.

The Newsround team want to know what you think and feel about issues that have an impact on your daily lives. Kids' opinions are just as important as those of adults. So in putting this book together, we thought it would be great for you to have some space to write your own stories, or to stick information or newspaper cuttings that have made an impact on you, or that you just like.

You could stick your own photographs on these pages too, or use the space to draw something. Really it is up to you... they are YOUR pages. For all you budding reporters, turn to the following pages, and get writing...!

Josh Braddock, 13, lives in an eco-home in Lanzarote with his parents and three siblings aged 7, 10 and 12.

Boats and palm trees in Lanzarote.

My parents are British but have lived on the island for 20 years, so I was born here. They came here because they wanted to live a better, cleaner life, so they built our house out of natural stone and wood on 30,000 m² of land, along with other properties which we rent out to holiday-makers who want to experience eco-tourism. All the houses use the latest renewable energy systems so we have 30 solar panels and wind turbines which generate our energy from the sun and the wind. We grow a lot of our own food and keep chickens for eggs. I love living like this, and think we should all do what we can to help the environment.

LET'S TALK ABOUT THE NEWS

Here is the news… about the news. It matters. Why? Well, it's part of human nature to be curious. We want to know about the universe and the planet we live on, our own race, other species and anything which might affect our lives. A piece of information can be called 'newsworthy' if it is new and if it will interest us. Media organisations in the UK - which own the newspapers we read, the radio and TV programmes we tune into and the websites we log on to – set their own news 'agenda', deciding which stories will be most relevant and interesting for their audience or readers. The amount of time or space given to a particular story therefore varies from channel to channel, paper to paper. Before deciding to run a story, journalists, editors and producers will ask themselves questions like: is this ground-breaking? Is it the first of something? Will it affect a lot of people? Who might those people be? Does this story have the power to entertain, intrigue or shock?

CHANGING FACE OF THE NEWS

Before the invention of the printing press in the 15th century, the only way to find out what was going on was from someone with a loud voice in the town square. Town Criers called out important information to the public – most of whom could neither read, nor write. The printing press however, made it possible to circulate information on paper and the first newspapers were born. The oldest independent national British newspaper still in existence is *The Times* which was first published in 1785. Since then, each technological advance has heralded a new and exciting way of receiving the news, from radio, to television to the advent of the internet. Today we live in such an 'instant' society that we want and expect to be continually kept up to date wherever we are. We can get ticker tape or pop up News Alerts at a computer. News Feeds or RSS (Really Simple Syndication) allow us to see when websites have added new content. We can even stay informed when we're out and about, via SMS (Simple Message Service) texts to our mobile phones.

TWO WAY NEWS

Citizen journalism: good news or bad?

Remember all those underground pictures of the London 7/7 bombings? They were all taken by people who happened to be there and who managed to snap a picture with their mobile phone or camera. Technology has allowed us all to interact with and contribute to the news; we don't need training, we just need the means to circulate what we see to a wider audience. This is known as 'citizen journalism' and some people believe it is dangerous because, unlike journalists, individual contributors don't understand the importance of **objectivity** when reporting an event. However many think UGC (user-generated content) is vital because, however large or comprehensive a news organisation is, it's impossible for them to be everywhere in the world. So where, once, a news story might have been missed or delayed due to lack of trained journalists on the ground, now ordinary people can ensure we know what's happening. For example, within 24 hours of the July 2007 bombings the BBC had received 1,000 stills and videos, 3,000 texts and 20,000 emails. That day, one piece on the BBC Six O'clock News was produced entirely from user-generated content.

WHEN 'REAL PEOPLE' BREAK THE NEWS

Two recent news stories which have been broken around the world with help from images taken by 'ordinary' people are:

An airliner ditching in the Hudson River, New York: In January 2009, a US Airways plane crash-landed in the Hudson after a flock of birds flew into its engine. Janis Krums was on a ferry which came to its aid and took the first photo of survivors crowded onto its wings. He posted it onto the Twitter website and within hours it was picked up by news desks around the world.

The baby dropped 40ft from a burning building: In February 2008 a fire engulfed a block of flats in Ludwigshafen, Germany, trapping the inhabitants. Sixty people were injured and nine died, including five children. However, one baby miraculously survived when he was dropped from the top floor down to waiting firemen. Passer-by Rene Werse, 43, captured the moment the baby was thrown.

HOW CAN WE TRUST THE NEWS?

Ever heard someone say 'never trust what you read in the papers'? In fact those who make the news have a huge responsibility to ensure that what they report is accurate and this is something they take very seriously. Journalists have to check and double check their sources and ensure they give a balanced account by offering both sides of the story. Behind the scenes, Newspapers and TV channels also have legal departments dedicated to ensuring the reliability of what they publish or broadcast. Adam Cannon is Group Legal Advisor for Associated Newspapers which owns the *Daily Mail*, *Mail on Sunday* and *Evening Standard*. He says, 'Print and Broadcast media are bound by strict codes which give them guidelines about what they can and can't do. If something a newspaper prints breaches the PCC Code of Practice in some way by misleading the public or misrepresenting a story, they can get into big trouble, they could be fined or have to pay thousands or millions of pounds in damages and ultimately it might damage their reputation. So the last thing an editor wants to do is to print something that's false. Around 70% of the articles written for the paper are seen by the legal team. We check if something is libelous, whether it invades someone's privacy, whether it infringes copyright or could damage a court case. We even have to check things like trademarks – that we don't call something a Hoover rather than a vacuum cleaner.'

FIVE GOLDEN RULES FOR GOOD JOURNALISM

1 **Answer the 5 'W' questions**
Check your story answers WHO, WHAT, WHERE, WHEN and WHY? For example: Who is the story about; What have they done? Where did they do it; Where and Why did it happen?

2 **Don't bury the best bits**
Make sure you put the most interesting and important parts of the story at the beginning. Ask yourself: Am I sure my readers will get this far?

3 **Research, don't guess**
Always do your research and start by making sure the issue really exists. Great journalists don't play with people's minds or make up problems. They investigate, analyse and tell.

4 **Be objective**
When writing try to see the issue from all sides. If it's a conflict situation, talk to both parties. If only one person is being interviewed you may still have to offer the other a right of reply.

5 **Learn what you are writing about**
A good journalist can write about just anything. Learn what you're writing and commit it to memory, that way if a related story occurs in future you'll be one step ahead.

NEWS THAT SHOCKS

Sometimes troubling news hits the headlines. Some of the more controversial and shocking stories over the past year include:

- The kidnapping of Shannon Matthews by family members
- Scientists warning effects on the climate from global warming are 'irreversible'
- The death of young Reality TV star Jade Goody from cancer
- Knife-crime and unprovoked murders of teenagers such as Jimmy Mizen

Consultant Clinical Psychologist David Trickey says:

'Although stories such as those listed above caused a lot of activity on the NR forums, the severity of an event is not actually a good predictor of who will be distressed. Different things upset different people, so you may find yourself being upset by something that doesn't seem to bother other people and equally wonder why others have found a particular story so distressing.

Stories that we hear in the news can affect the way that we think and feel in lots of different ways. Some will make us think that there are some really good people out there, and that might make us feel happy. Others might make us think that something excellent is going to happen soon, which might make us feel excited. Occasionally reports might make us think that we are in danger and that might make us feel scared, or an item might make us think about someone who has died or lost something that they wanted, and that might make us feel sad. These feelings are normal. In fact they are what make us human beings. The fact that we are able to love someone brings us lots of happiness, but when that person leaves or dies that makes us feel sad. You can't have one without the other. So if you or your friends are very upset by a particular news story, don't worry about the fact that you are upset – it's only natural. But if you find yourself getting very upset, or staying upset for quite a while, or the upset staying with you all the time, or maybe stopping you doing fun and important things that you would normally do, then you need to find some ways to make you feel better.'

For tips and advice on what to do if you're upset by the news turn to page 126.

Extreme weather

WHITE OUT

Presspackers all over the UK were thrilled by the record-breaking week of snowfall at the beginning of February 2009. The snow cover reached 15cm in places. The Arctic weather was so severe that councils closed thousands of schools across Britain, although the South East was worst hit. London buses were taken off the road and trains cancelled in what was to be the region's worst snowfall in 18 years.

FROZEN FACTS

- On Monday 2nd February 2009, more snow fell in Britain in a day than in most of the world's ski resorts!

- Congestion charging in London was suspended for the first Monday of the snows due to 'challenging conditions'.

- The longest traffic queue caused by the weather was on the M25, with tailbacks stretching over 87 kilometres long!

- Temperatures plummeted to -6°C, while the wind chill factor hit -20°C at times.

- At least a million kids didn't have to go to school for up to a week during the freeze!

- One in five people took a 'snow day' off from work.

- When the ice finally melted, many parts of the UK also suffered from severe flooding.

School's out! Children all over the country enjoyed the unexpected time off school, to play out in the snow and go sledging down the streets, while the government struggled to keep the nation running.

KNOW YOUR STUFF

How did Britain cope?

As the cold snap continued, many parts of the UK struggled to clear roads and keep services up and running. Countries in Scandinavia deal with much heavier snowfall every winter, so why did the chill cause such chaos over here? It seems that the weather was so unusual, the authorities simply weren't equipped to cope.

Out of salt

Gritters spread brown rock salt across the road to melt the snow and prevent black ice from setting in. As the big chill continued, councils used up most of their supplies – forcing them to ration gritting or turn to other materials such as white table salt.

Not enough ploughs

Because this level of snow was so unusual, there weren't enough snowploughs to clear the roads. Vital agencies such as the ambulances and mobile meals services had problems reaching the people that needed them.

Power down

The snow was so extreme in areas like Somerset and the North of England, power lines were cut off. Many people had to make do without electricity or gas until it was possible to get to the cables and repair them.

In the news

The extreme conditions were caused by Arctic winds sweeping across from Siberia and the East, combined with rain coming into the country from the South. This meant that much of Europe also had to endure the same bitter temperatures and heavy snowfalls.

Afghanistan endured its worst winter for 30 years.

• PRESS PACK REPORT •

'The snow was about half a metre deep!'

'We live in a rural village in Oxfordshire. I'd seen snow a few times, but when I opened the curtains one day in February I couldn't believe it. It had drifted up against the back door and the roads were blocked so no one could get in or out of the village for four days. The village shop ran out of everything like bread, milk and eggs and there were no newspapers. On the first day we also had a long power cut so there was no TV or anything, but my brother and sister and I didn't mind because we were outside anyway. It was brilliant – we had the week off school and we had fun sledging and making massive snowmen.'
Joe Tosh, 10, Steeple Aston, Oxfordshire.

more about why and how the weather changes as it does.

BLAZE IN THE AUSTRALIAN BUSH

In February 2009 Australia endured the deadliest bush fires in recorded history. The southern state of Victoria was masked in thick smoke as flames tore through towns and villages at a terrifying pace. Over 200 people were killed, with a further 5,000 made homeless as fires destroyed their cars and property. Tens of thousands of firefighters battled for several days to try and stop the blazes spreading further. Fires also broke out in the states of New South Wales and South Australia, but these were smaller or located in areas away from people. Bush fires happen naturally in hot and dry places, but it is believed that a long drought combined with high winds and temperatures of 47°C caused the fires to spiral out of control.

Firefighters battle the flames to try and stop the fires spreading.

• PRESS PACK REPORT •

'Trying to contain the bush fires was dangerous work.'

'One of my mum's good friends is called Tom. He lives in Victoria, Australia, and volunteers for the D.S.E (The Department of Sustainability and Environment). It is a government agency for the management of water resources, climate change, bush fires, public land, forests and ecosystems. When the bush fires started Tom trained so that he could help put them out. He was responsible for 'blacking out', which means making sure that the areas which have been burnt out by fire stay burnt out. Tom and my mum stay in touch by email and so we heard all about it. There was even an article on the Internet from his local newspaper about his work in the Bunyip State Park.It sounds like he was very brave. People were describing it as 'hell' and he said that he'd worked three shifts in a row. I felt proud of him and glad that we don't really get things like that happening over here. Hundreds of people lost their homes or died.'

Alex Milne, 11, Cambridgeshire.

Ricky Boleto surveys the devastating bush fire damage.

Did you know?

With more than 1,600 houses razed to the ground, relief centres were quickly set up to shelter the victims.

The Australian Army also opened up some of its bases for people to stay in. Each centre offered clean water, food and clothes plus a noticeboard to help people find missing family or neighbours. Many companies also donated money or gifts to those that had lost everything. Newsround's Ricky Boleto visited Whittlesea Support Centre (see photographs left), about 50 kilometres outside Melbourne. He was surprised at how cheerful the mood was despite everything the residents had gone through. It will be months before the worst affected towns can be rebuilt, although some Victorians have vowed never to go back.

KNOW YOUR STUFF

How fire spreads

Even though the fire service and the Australian Army did everything they could to get people to safety, not everyone was able to escape in time. Witnesses said that their houses were engulfed with flames that stretched 50 metres into the air. There were also reports of explosions as fuel and gas supplies ignited.

Although many people started making escape plans as soon as they spotted smoke in the distance, it was very hard for them to judge how fast the fire was moving. This is because instead of covering ground at a constant speed, flames travel in pulses. Experts say that a burning fire will periodically stop for a few moments, before suddenly covering a few hundred metres at an incredibly fast pace. The parched Victoria countryside burnt like a tinder paper, devouring villages before they could be cleared.

Fires of this size do not have to touch in order to burn. With flames reaching a scorching hot 1,000 °C, damage can be caused to objects 200 metres away. The fires also throw out scalding hot gases and embers.

How did it all start?

Spot fires break out every year in hot and dry areas like the Australian eucalyptus forests. Some begin naturally, while others are the result of human activity. Here are the main causes:

WEB CHECK For more news go to www.abc.net.au/news/events/bushfires/stories.htm

Lightning strikes
Many bush fires are sparked when a lightning bolt strikes the ground, igniting dry branches or undergrowth.

Careless in the countryside
Some people start fires without even thinking. Dropped cigarettes or barbecues that haven't been put out properly can relight and spread all too quickly.

Electrical meltdown
When power cables are exposed to extreme hot weather they can melt or burst into flame.

Arson
Sometimes people start fires on purpose. This dangerous and criminal activity is called arson.

In the news

California burning

In November 2008 a state of emergency was declared in four areas of California. The countryside was ablaze with what Americans call 'wildfires' – fanned out of control by warm desert winds. Planes and helicopters worked day and night to water-bomb the flames, but over 800 homes were burnt out.

Animals in danger

More than a million Australian animals got caught up in the fires too.
Many people at the relief centres said that the flames approached so fast, they had no choice but to leave their pets behind. Vets worked round the clock to save patients suffering from burnt paws and smoke inhalation. Wildlife centres also struggled to cope with rescued koalas, kangaroos, lizards and birds.

A koala is given a drink of water by a Country Fire Authority volunteer afer he rescued her following the deadly bush fires that swept through Miraboo North, an area about 120km southeast of Melbourne.

SINKING CITIES

The last twelve months saw floods drench even normally dry countries like Australia and Morocco. Venice also experienced a soggy December in 2008, with sea levels rising over 1.56 metres higher than normal. The lagoon city suffered its worst flood since 1986 and forced over 3,000 residents to seek higher ground. A special underwater dam that will protect the city is planned for 2011.

People had to wade through the flooded streets and squares of Venice.

Flood calendar

January 2008
Eastern Australia experiences worst flooding in 20 years. Southern Africa is flooded, with thousands made homeless in Malawi, Zambia and Zimbabwe.

May 2008
Thousands flee homes in Colombia, where it has been raining since March.

June 2008
The worst rainy season in southern China for half a century takes the lives of at least 57, with more than 1.25 million fleeing their homes. India's extreme monsoon rains cause the worst flood devastation in 60 years. The worst affected areas are Orissa and West Bengal.

October 2008
Flash floods in eastern and southern Morocco, are the most extreme in 30 years.

Wet weather warning?

What causes flooding and other types of extreme weather, such as prolonged drought and unseasonal snow?

Many scientists believe that climate change could be influencing weather all over the world to at least some degree. When they study the weather, scientists discount the odd blip like the snows of February 2009. Instead they study much longer patterns, such as increases in temperature that show up again and again during the course of years.

Experts agree that global warming is likely to lead to further flooding in the future. A report in June 2008 also advised that the government needs to construct more dams and flood defences to protect the UK.

KNOW YOUR STUFF

Staying safe
When heavy rains fall, remember these top tips for staying safe:

1. Watch the weather forecasts
2. Seal any gaps with waterproof tape
3. Move valuable objects upstairs
4. Look out for pets and animals
5. Keep calm

Rainy days for the UK

After the record-breaking summer floods of 2007, many children and their families faced the start of 2008 without their home or possessions.

Tewkesbury had been so badly affected hundreds of people were still forced to live in caravans or stay with relatives over a year later. In July 2008 thousands of people joined hands around the Abbey to remember the calamity of the year before.

A freak hailstorm on 30th October 2008 saw over 100 millimetres ice pelt down in a few hours, plunging the Devon town of Ottery St Mary into chaos. Flash flooding in December also caused traffic chaos in southern England, Wales and Scotland.

One way only - by boat! Roads all over the country were flooded during the terrible storms of 2008.

Active planet!

KIDS ON CLIMATE CHANGE

Last year hundreds of presspackers all over the world wrote into Newsround to share their worries about the environment. It is now widely agreed that the level of greenhouse gases that man produces are indeed warming up the Earth's atmosphere, triggering massive changes in its weather patterns. What isn't as easy to measure is when these changes will happen and how drastic their effects will be. Unfortunately, floods and droughts, animals becoming extinct and melting icecaps are already signs of global warming. The good news however, is that scientists believe that it's not too late to try and do something to help. Children are especially important, because they are the next generation of adults with the power to safeguard the fragile future of our world.

SHOCKING FACTS

- Some experts now believe that the Amazon rainforest could shrink by 85% during the next century if the world doesn't stop polluting the atmosphere at such a fast rate.

- Scientists in March 2009 found that climate change was also damaging the world's oceans. A study of tiny sea creatures showed that increased carbon dioxide in the water meant they weren't growing as fast as they used to.

- If nothing is done to reverse global warming, sea levels could rise by 50 centimetres in the next few decades, exposing almost twice as many people to the risk of severe flooding.

- Many wonderful plant and animal species all over the world are now at risk of dying out because their habitats are shrinking as a result of climate change. The list includes polar bears and reef-building coral.

Frozen beauty. Sea levels will rise dangerously as the Earth's icecaps continue to melt.

TAKE ACTION TODAY! Kids can make a positive difference to climate change. Here are some ways you can make a change.

1 **Think before you throw it away**
Encourage your friends and family to recycle as much as they can. Take your glass, newspapers, tin cans, plastics and newspapers to recycling centres and save shopping bags. Mobile phones, ink cartridges and old clothing can all be reused too.

2 **Legs not revs**
Short car journeys are extremely damaging to the environment because engines pollute more when they are warming up. Make a difference by walking to school or getting on your bike. If you must go by car, try and share with a friend.

3 **Simply switch off!**
Turn off lights and gadgets when you leave the room. Make sure that TVs and stereos aren't left on standby and you'll immediately start to shrink your carbon footprint. You can even get clockwork mobile phone chargers!

4 **Shop sensibly**
Avoid buying products that are presented in loads of unnecessary packaging. If you're at the supermarket, choose food that has been grown locally rather than imported by air from the other side of the world.

Natural disasters

DEVASTATION IN SOUTH EAST ASIA

Reports showed that over 235,000 people died in 2008, making it one of the decade's worst years for natural disasters. On May 2nd Cyclone Nargis tore through Burma. The terrible storm claimed approximately 100,000 lives, with thousands more declared missing. Ten days later the Sichuan province of China was rocked by a huge earthquake registering 8.0 on the Richter Scale. Later in the year, earthquakes in Pakistan left 300 dead.

Classroom devastation. Viewers all over the world gasped to see images on their computer and TV screens of Chinese school children trapped under fallen buildings

Tragedy in Sichuan

At 2.28pm on May 12th 2008, China was struck by its most powerful earthquake in over 30 years.

The epicentre of the disaster was in Beichuan county, over 1,500 kilometres away from the capital of Beijing. The quake was so massive however, workers in the city reported feeling the ground shake for over two minutes at the same time that the first tremors hit.

The earthquake happened in the early afternoon, so most children were still at school. Thousands of pupils got trapped under the rubble of classrooms as buildings collapsed and giant holes formed in the ground. President Hu Jintao called for an 'all-out effort' to help recover the victims, but around 70,000 lost their lives.

Almost three months after the quake, Sonali Shah travelled to China for the opening of the Beijing Olympics. Even then, the country was reeling from the quake. She met families still living in tents, waiting for their homes, hospitals and schools to be rebuilt.

In the news

Turbulent Earth

The world was plagued with other natural disasters in 2008. In February at least 55 were declared dead when a tornado ripped through southern USA. In June, Typhoon Fengshen hit the Philippines, causing flash floods and landslides. In October, there was an earthquake in Pakistan, 70 kilometres north of Quetta. The tremors reached a magnitude of 6.4 and took the lives of 170 people.

The eye of the storm - a satellite image of a hurricane.

KNOW YOUR STUFF

Were Cyclone Nargis and the Sichuan Earthquake linked?

The two Asian disasters took place within the same fortnight, but scientists say that they were just a dreadful coincidence. Cyclone Nargis began out in the ocean as a tropical storm, before sweeping into land. The Chinese earthquake was caused when two of the Earth's plates bashed together deep underground, sending powerful vibrations up to the surface.

Storm quiz

'Typhoon', 'hurricane' and 'cyclone' are just names that people in different parts of the world use to describe a tropical storm. Take this quiz to test how good your windy weather knowledge is...

1 Hurricanes are storms that appear...
   a. Over the Pacific Ocean.
   b. Over the North Atlantic Ocean.
   c. Over the Mediterranean.

2 Tropical storms that build up over the Pacific Ocean are known as...
   a. Typhoons
   b. Twisters
   c. Monsoons

3 Storms are given names like Nargis because...
   a. It helps people to tell them apart.
   b. It's a tradition in tropical countries.
   c. Scientists ran out of numbers.

4 The southern states of the USA are regularly struck by...
   a. Earthquakes
   b. Tornadoes
   c. Cyclones

5 Scientists choose how to name storms by...
   a. picking their favourite baby names.
   b. selecting names for the year in alphabetical order.
   c. pulling random names out of a hat.

Answers: 1b, 2a, 3a, 4b, 5b

ALL CREATURES GREAT AND SMALL

Sometimes animals make the news for sad or upsetting reasons. All too often we hear accounts of cruelty to wildlife, extinction and freak attacks on humans. Luckily some recent headlines have been more upbeat for animal-loving presspackers. Since 2008 a horde of new fascinating species have been discovered across the globe. The prize for animal superstar of the year however, has to go to an old favourite – the giant panda.

Pandas in the press

Four new panda cubs
At the end of July, four baby giant pandas were born within 14 hours of each other. The cubs were born at Chengdu Panda Breeding Research Centre in Sichuan, China.

Cuddly Christmas presents
In the past, China has had a frosty relationship with nearby Taiwan. All that is set to change now, thanks to a gift of two giant pandas. The Chinese government presented the bears to Taiwan as a gesture of renewed friendship in December 2008. The pandas are called Tuan Tuan and Yuan Yuan because 'tuanyuan' means 'reunion' in Chinese.

The giant panda is one of the world's most endangered species. Experts believe that there are only about 1,600 now left living in the wild.

ANIMAL NEWCOMERS!

Researchers are always trying to record new facts about the animals that share our planet. Unearthing even the tiniest new bug can reveal all sorts of secrets about how the natural world works! Here are some of their most exciting discoveries...

1 A new insect for China
Scientists were jumping for joy when they found a brand new insect hiding in the rainforests of Yinggeling Nature Reserve in January 2009. The bug was given the catchy name *Dolichothyreus stigmatus*.

2 Ten chirruping tree frogs
In Spring 2009, an environmental group announced that it had found no less than ten types of tree frogs in the mountains of Columbia. Every single one is believed to be new to science.

3 Spider as big as a plate
The Greater Mekong is a vast Asian rainforest that has offered up over a thousand new species during the last ten years. Perhaps the most scary is the *Heteropoda maxima* spider. This cave-dwelling giant measures 30 centimetres across!

4 Stripy bouncing fish
Scuba divers off the island of Ambon in East Indonesia discovered a strange tan and peach fish hiding in the coral. The never-seen-before froglike creature bounces along the ocean floor just like a rubber ball.

5 Reef prawns
A worldwide survey that aims to list the names of every living thing in the ocean has found all sorts of new corals and marine animals in the Great Barrier Reef. The biggest are shrimp-like creatures with claws that are longer than their bodies.

Museum mammoth

In October 2008 the Natural History Museum in London unveiled a record-breaking new exhibit – the longest insect in the world. The stick insect, called *Phobaeticus chani*, measures over 56 centimetres from antennae to toe. The rare bug comes from the rainforests of Borneo. It's commonly called 'Chan's Megastick', named after the naturalist who found it.

Croc out of control!

Very occasionally, humans become the victims of animals.

Crocodile rarely hunt people, but in April 2008 a man managed to rescue his wife when a saltwater croc lunged for her in an Australian national park. Norm Pretherick leapt on the reptile's back then poked it in the eye, forcing it to unclench its jaws.

Endangered!

A HELPING HAND FOR GORILLAS

Every year an organisation called the International Union for Conservation (IUCN) draws up a list of the world's most endangered species. The 'Red List' as it is known, features many thousands of at risk animals, including primates from Africa and Asia. Happily however, 2008 brought good news for apes. In August experts were thrilled to discover two huge new groups of western lowland gorillas living in the Republic of Congo. Over 100,000 of the shy creatures were counted, offering a massive improvement to the originally recorded numbers. Over in Cameroon, a special reserve was set up to protect and breed the rare Cross River gorilla.

ENDANGERED MAMMALS

Today, one out of every four mammals is threatened with extinction. This means that more mammals are endangered today than ever before, as their homes or food sources disappear. Here are some unlucky species teetering on the edge:

1 Vancouver Island marmot
This curious North American rodent can only be found in one small patch of land. It is believed that there are less than 40 left.

2 Black rhino
The rhino has been a victim of poaching for years. Right now the population is starting to grow again, but numbers still only reach about 4,000.

3 Iberian lynx
Only 150 of these wild cats still prowl parts of Spain. This Lynx is disappearing fast because the type of rabbit it feeds on is also dying out.

4 Baiji (or Yangtze) dolphin
This Chinese dolphin is now so rare scientists believe that it may possibly be extinct already.

5 Tasmanian devil
This little black creature with long whiskers is growing rarer and rarer. The main cause of its decline is a nasty illness that is sweeping through the population.

KNOW YOUR STUFF

Disappearing worlds

It's not just animals that are endangered, some of their most precious habitats are shrinking fast too. In June 2008 shocking satellite photos snapped over Africa showed how drastically the continent had changed during the last 35 years. The once vast Lake Chad in West Africa had shrunk to one tenth of its original size. The pictures also showed that lots of ice had melted from the top of the world's highest Mountain, Kilimanjaro. Experts think that one of the reasons why the continent has got so badly damaged is because Africa's total population has now doubled to a staggering total of 965 million.

The Galapagos Islands that lie off Ecuador in South America are just as important. The scattered islands are famous for their giant tortoises, but many more rare species take refuge in the remote forests and beaches. In June 2008 the world held its breath when the Cerro Azul volcano on Isabela Island erupted. The crater spewed lava for four days, but luckily no harm was done to the Galapagos.

PROTECTING BRITISH WILDLIFE

Not all species under threat are found in far away places!

In February 2009, the Saving Scotland's Red Squirrel (SSRS) project was launched. Since the introduction of the grey squirrel in the 1800s, reds have got fewer and fewer. This is partly because grey squirrels carry a nasty disease called squirrel pox that can kill a red squirrel in less than two weeks. Most of the UK's remaining reds live in Scotland, with current numbers standing at 121,000.

THE FALL AND RISE OF THE WHALE

Naturalists were pleased to discover in August 2008 that there was a rise in the reported numbers of Humpback and Southern Right Whales. This might be due to a ban in hunting. Whales also made the headlines when in March 2008 over 80 long-finned pilot whales and bottlenose dolphins got stranded on a beach in south west Australia. Many died, but experts were hopeful of rescuing at least some of the group.

Your environment and nature

You could also stick or clip, newspaper cuttings or pictures that you'd like to keep.

33

Sonali Shah

1 Describe your path into presenting Newsround?
After studying Broadcast Journalism at University, I got a job as a breakfast news presenter on a radio station called Sunrise Radio. I then moved to the BBC World Service, where I worked mainly in business news. After that, I became a money reporter for BBC Radio 5 Live, before sending a tape of myself to Newsround. Luckily for me, they saw some potential!

2 Which of the past year's news stories particularly struck a chord with you?
The terror attacks in Mumbai. I was in India just before they happened and had to fly back into Mumbai airport when the gunmen were still shooting. When I'm in Mumbai on holiday, I usually stay or socialise at the hotels that were attacked. It's sad to see something like that happening to places you know so well.

3 Was there anything you found difficult to cover and how do you cope with negative or distressing stories?
I think explaining the global financial crisis to our audience is difficult – but we did it well. Some people may think talking about the economy would bore an eight year old, but if you explain stuff in a simple and engaging way, it isn't boring. The world's money problems affect everyone, so why shouldn't everyone know about it?

Just before the 2008 Olympics, we filmed a Newsround special on the earthquake in China. We met families who had lost everything but were still smiling – it's moving to see people coping so well in a bad situation. It reminds you not to sweat the small stuff.

4 What has been the biggest news story you've ever covered and what made it so important?
The 2008 Beijing Olympics was the biggest assignment I've ever had. It was billed as the biggest show on earth and being there, it certainly felt like that. With more than 200 countries taking part and so many sports, there were so many stories – just not enough time to cover them all.

Sonali in China.

Sonali at the Beijing Olympics.

5 **What do you do in a typical day?**
I present our bulletins most days. If I'm presenting the early ones, I'm in at 6am and it's straight into action – we discuss what's going on around the world, decide what we want in the programme, write scripts, cut pictures and I put on some make-up for our first update at 7am. After the final update at 8.25am, I either go out filming or work on scripts for the next day. If I'm presenting our afternoon bulletins, I usually get assigned a story in the morning. We start looking for pictures, interviewees, places to film. We begin writing scripts and then go out to film. More often than not, it's a race against time to get it all done before I need to go into make-up for the bulletins.

6 **What's the most exciting thing about your job?**
Never knowing what you're going to be working on or who you're going to meet next.

7 **Are there any downsides to being a news reporter/presenter?**
I can't think of any. My days always tend to be super busy, but I like that.

8 **Have you had any on-screen disasters so far?**
There have been times when tapes haven't run when they should have in the programme and I wasn't quite sure what was going on. One of those times, fellow presenter Adam and I started talking about chips! I'm not quite sure why?

A new US president

OBAMA MOVES INTO THE WHITE HOUSE

On a wintry Tuesday in January 2009, Barack Obama was sworn in as the 44th President of America. He stood outside the US Capitol Building in Washington DC to make a promise called the Oath of Office. Outgoing leader George W Bush was there to take part in the ceremony, as well as a record-breaking crowd of over a million well-wishers. Obama's election is seen as especially important because he is the United States' first ever black president.

America celebrates in front of the US Capitol Building as Barack Obama is sworn in as the 44th President of America.

The race to Washington

Winning the presidential elections marks the end of a very long journey for Obama.

Obama is a member of the Democrat party. Before he was even allowed to run for President, he had to beat rival candidate Hillary Clinton. It was a tough, drawn-out battle because Mrs Clinton had lots of experience and a strong set of supporters. As the wife of ex-president Bill Clinton, she also had the advantage of being a former First Lady. In June 2008, Obama's stirring speeches and determination to change the way the USA is run, finally helped him win the candidacy.

Once he was ready to fight for office, Obama found himself up against Republican candidate John McCain. McCain was a respected war hero. Obama and McCain's fiercest clashes were over the conflict in Iraq – McCain was a staunch supporter whilst Obama wanted American soldiers to withdraw from the war zone.

On November 4th 2008, Obama defeated McCain in the election. Barack greeted his supporters with an acceptance speech saying: "It's been a long time coming, but tonight change has come to America."

TOP TEN

The Obama files – 10 surprising facts about the US President

1 He collects *Conan The Barbarian* and *Spider-Man* comics and recently appeared in issue #583 of 'Marvel's Amazing Spider-Man'.

2 He worked in a Baskin-Robbins ice-cream shop as a teenager and now can't stand ice-cream.

3 He was known as 'Barry' until he went to University and asked to be addressed by his full name.

4 He won a Grammy Award in 2006 for the spoken word version of his memoir, 'Dreams From My Father'.

5 He is left-handed – the sixth president to be left-handed since the Second World War.

6 His name means 'one who is blessed' in Swahili.

7 He's into the same books and music as his kids. He's read every Harry Potter story and enjoys playing hip-hop tracks.

8 He would have liked to have been an architect if he hadn't become a politician.

9 He carries good luck charms with him – a tiny Madonna and child statue and a bracelet belonging to a soldier in Iraq.

10 He's not perfect. He says his worst habit is constantly checking his BlackBerry.

After studying law at one of America's top universities, Obama worked as a lawyer for people's rights before getting into politics.

KNOW YOUR STUFF
Why Obama matters

The new President's election represents a major landmark in black history. Around the time that the USA was first founded, thousands of African-Americans were being bought and sold as slaves. These people lived in great poverty, stripped of the right to choose their own destiny. Slavery was abolished in 1865, but it took nearly a hundred years before black people in America were given the same treatment as their white countrymen. Black and white children were sent to separate schools. Along the way many brave campaigners suffered and even died in protest against this inequality.

By taking the most powerful job in the USA, Barack Obama has shown the world how much things have changed for black people since the days of the slave trade.

Adam visited the 'Oval office' at an exhibition about US presidents, while he was in Washington for the election.

Newsround's Adam Fleming was at the centre of action during the run-up to the final election for the 44th US President. He was up for 30 hours during election night, talking to people and watching history being made as the votes came in.

• PRESS PACK REPORT •

'It is nice to see a President who looks like he could be part of my family.'
'I was one of the hundreds of people celebrating Obama's election win at the Drum (The National Centre for Black British Arts and Culture) in Birmingham. There was a fantastic party atmosphere and everyone was smiling and hugging each other. This has been a special time for me and my family. I'm British but my grandparents came here from Jamaica and have told me a lot about black history and the struggle to be seen as equal. Obama makes me think that if I work hard I can be anything I want to be.'

Rhema Howell-Smith, 8, Birmingham.

COOL FACTS
LIFE IN THE WHITE HOUSE

The new President, Barack Obama with the First Lady, Michelle Obama, and their two daughters, Sasha and Malia.

What is daily life really like for America's First Family?

- The President says lack of exercise makes him 'cranky' so first thing in the morning he shoots hoops on the basketball court he's installed in his new home. He can also be found in the in-house gym for an hour each day before beginning his duties.

- Barack Obama's daughters, Sasha, seven, and Malia, 10, go to school every day, but don't have to brave public transport or the school bus. They travel in a motorcade guarded by Secret Service agents.

- The Obamas are the most guarded family on the planet. Security around the President is so tight that bodyguards accompany him everywhere – even standing outside the lavatory!

- Mum Michelle has a lot to think about – besides her duties as First Lady she has a budget of £150,000 to redecorate the 132 room residence.

- The First Family certainly don't spend time cleaning their rooms! They have more than 100 domestic staff including florists, drivers and even dressers who help them pick out clothes.

- The family try to eat together whenever possible and have 25 chefs to prepare their meals. At the weekends the Obama girls enjoy White House sleepovers with friends from school and every Sunday morning the family go to church.

Did you know?

The Obamas have the use of a yacht called The Sequoia if they want to go on a sailing holiday. They can also relax and ski at the Presidential retreat, Camp David, in Maryland.

KNOW YOUR STUFF

Can Obama live up to the hype?

After all the excitement of Obama's campaign, can he really fulfil our expectations? Once they come to power politicians are often accused of forgetting about their pre-election promises.

What he promised:

- To withdraw troops from Iraq within 16 months and to continue the battle against Al-Qaeda and the Taliban in Afghanistan.

- To close Guantánamo Bay, a prison where suspected terrorists are currently being kept without trial.

- To increase the minimum wage – the lowest amount that employers are allowed to pay people who work for them.

- To reform the healthcare system so that the 47 million Americans who cannot afford insurance will be able to get medicine and treatment.

- To make America a world leader in environmental issues and head the search for alternative sources of energy.

- To regulate the banking system.

What he's done so far:

- Directed his government to close down Guantánemo Bay within one year and forbidden US government agents to torture prisoners.

- Signed a bill so that the government will pay for health insurance for children whose parents cannot afford it.

- Pulled the plug on huge bonuses for failing bankers. Bosses of banks which the government has had to help out can no longer received super-sized pay cheques.

- Begun addressing green issues on a variety of fronts.

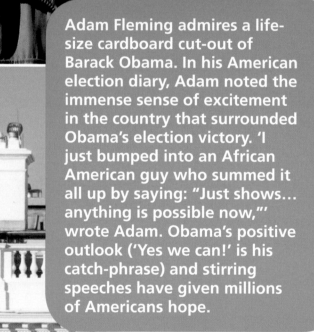

Adam Fleming admires a life-size cardboard cut-out of Barack Obama. In his American election diary, Adam noted the immense sense of excitement in the country that surrounded Obama's election victory. 'I just bumped into an African American guy who summed it all up by saying: "Just shows… anything is possible now,"' wrote Adam. Obama's positive outlook ('Yes we can!' is his catch-phrase) and stirring speeches have given millions of Americans hope.

• PRESS PACK REPORT •

'I think he will definitely be better than Bush.'

'I'm half American and my whole family watched the inauguration ceremony on the news. My older brother is mixed race – we have different Dads – so I think it was especially important for him. When we lived in Virginia there was a lot of racism, much more than here. I remember my brother being sad because other boys at his school bullied him because he wasn't black or white. So maybe having someone of mixed race leading the country will bring people together. I also like Obama's ideas on Iraq as my Dad is in the Air Force and I would hate it if he was sent out there.'

Rose Linton, 12, Ely, Cambridgeshire.

Old and young were out on the streets of Washington to hear Obama's acceptance speech.

The White House – home of the First Family.

EXIT FROM IRAQ

Sadly it seems that there are always some countries in the world that are at war at any one time. Last year, conflicts were raging in many places across the globe from Africa to the Middle East. Many British troops continued to be deployed in Afghanistan and Iraq during 2008. But while the Afghanistan situation looks set to continue for some time, in March 2009 British troops began to withdraw from Iraq after six years of fighting. After the 4,000 or so members of the Army have finally returned to the UK, around 400 will stay on to help Iraqi forces keep the peace in the country.

KNOW YOUR STUFF

Countries in conflict

Countries clash over many issues, but war often breaks out when nations disagree about the land that they own. In some hotspots, people have fought on and off for years – divided by their nationality, religion or way of life. Here are two of the most troubled news stories of 2008...

In March, authorities fired on crowds during protests in Tibet. The territory is ruled by China, but most people in Tibet are desperate to bring back their leader, the Dalai Lama, and govern themselves. No one officially knows how many people died during the riots, but the number may be as high as 2000.

The Israelis and Palestinians have been locked in a violent argument about the territory of Gaza, a tiny strip of land that lies between the Mediterranean Sea and Israel, for many years. In January 2009 the region was badly damaged in three weeks of bitter fighting.

British troops in Helmand Province in Afghanistan.

Afghanistan battles on

British forces have been in Afghanistan since 2001 and there is no sign of them leaving anytime soon. The country used to be ruled by a group called the Taliban, but the UK and USA invaded after they suspected that they were responsible for the 9/11 terrorist attacks in the USA. A new government was formed in Afghanistan, but the Taliban were determined to fight it. Unfortunately the country still remains a very troubled and dangerous place to live.

As part of its service in Afghanistan, the British Army works with 35 other countries as part of a peace-keeping group called the International Security Assistance Force (ISAF). The British soldiers have two goals:

1. Help the Afghanistan soldiers keep the country safe whilst rebuilding vital schools and hospitalls.

2. Destroy fields planted with illegal drugs that are harvested and sold overseas.

When President Obama came to power, the USA announced that it was rethinking its actions in Afghanistan. As a result extra troops and more support for the local people are going to be put in place.

Why not add your voice to the First News Conflict Children Campaign, the biggest ever schools project that aims to give children a voice in supporting kids caught up in the violence of war. The campaign is run in partnership with the Department for International Development (DFID) and Save the Children. See WEB CHECK at the bottom of the page for the website address to log on to for more information about this campaign.

In the news

The Soldier Prince

In February 2008 Prince Harry spent 10 weeks serving as a soldier in Afghanistan. As a member of the Household Cavalry he went on many foot patrols in an area called Helmand Province. So that he and the people around him could stay safe, his tour had to be kept a secret. The Prince planned to stay for longer, but unfortunately he had to come home when an American website told the world what he was doing. He received the Afghanistan medal in May 2008.

MUMBAI ATTACKS

Many presspackers were affected when they watched footage of smoke billowing out of the Taj Mahal hotel in November 2008. Mumbai fell into chaos when gunmen mounted attacks on seven separate locations within the city, including the busy Chhatrapati Shivaji Terminus railway station and Cama Hospital. The shooting lasted for three days, killing almost 200 and injuring at least 370. Many innocent people from different countries were caught up the violence, most finding themselves trapped in two of Mumbai's luxury hotels. While the army and special services fought to free the hostages, the masked attackers lobbed grenades and fired at the crowds.

A city under seige - Mumbai's Taj Mahal hotel was one of the targets of the terrorist attack.

KNOW YOUR STUFF

Who planned the Mumbai attacks?

The Indian government is still trying to work out who planned the attacks and why. At the time, a group called Deccan Mujahedeen said that they were responsible, but nobody really knew why they would want to carry out such violence against the city.

After they had done some more investigating, India accused a banned group called Lashkar-e-Taiba. This militant organisation is based in Pakistan. During the weeks after the shootings there were lots of arguments between the leaders of India and Pakistan. The Indian Prime Minister Manmohan Singh was convinced that Pakistani citizens were responsible for the terrible crimes. Most of the gunmen were killed during the attacks, but in February 2009 the only surviving terrorist was charged with 'waging war' against India. Pakistan has since admitted that the events were partly planned on its soil.

 PAGE 126 If news reports about war and terrorism make you feel anxious and upset, turn to

KNOW YOUR FACTS

How does terrorism affect you?

Ever since the New York twin towers were destroyed on September 11th 2001, the issue of terrorism has cropped up in the news again and again. The July 2007 bombings in London brought our fears even closer to home. Unfortunately terrorism isn't a new thing – it's been happening across the world for years.

Terrorism is when people use violence to make others behave the way that they want. Sometimes however, we aren't even clear about who has performed such an aggressive deed or why they felt driven to do it in the first place.

Although such cruel acts of terror make most of us feel frightened, it's important to remember that they are very rare. In the UK a huge network of government agencies, secret intelligence units and the police are working hard to protect us all. They stop many attacks before they have the chance to hit the headlines. Increasing the security we see in airports, public buildings and at stadium events also helps keep the country safe.

Cricket tour chaos

During the attacks in Mumbai, the England cricket team was on tour in India.

A few weeks' earlier, they had even stayed in one of the hotels later wrecked by the events of November 2008. After the news had broken, the team decided to postpone its final two one-day matches and leave the country until things calmed down. When they returned a few weeks' later, a minute's silence was held at the start of the first match, to remember the victims.

Sadly, in March 2009 a separate incident in Pakistan was set to cause more devastation. The Sri Lankan cricket team's tour bus was driving to a match in Lahore when it was fired on by a dozen armed terrorists. The vehicle was attacked by grenades and rocket launchers, killing eight people. The Sri Lankan wicket keeper Kumar Sangakkara said the team only managed to escape to the safety of the stadium thanks to the skill and nerve of the bus driver. No-one knows why the bus was fired on in this way.

A setback for Northern Ireland

After 30 years of unrest, the peace process in Northern Ireland was put under pressure when two soldiers were shot in March 2009. The two young men were killed when they came out to accept a pizza delivery at the Massereene Barracks in Antrim. It was the first fatal shooting in the region for 12 years, an act that Gordon Brown described as 'evil and cowardly'. Two days later a policeman was also killed in County Armagh. After the murders, thousands of people in Northern Ireland felt upset and angry. Many of them attended peace rallies to show their determination not to give in to terrorism.

page 126 to find out how to deal with these kind of stories.

Money, money, money!

THE SLIDE INTO RECESSION

Britain's been having a tough time recently, but it's not the only country to be struck with money worries. The credit crunch began in the USA during 2007, and unfortunately during the last 18 months things have only got worse. After the scare in the US, every nation in the world has been sliding deeper into a recession. After years of lending too much cash to people who didn't have the means to pay it back, banks decided to crack down on how much they were willing to lend. This meant there was less money around for ordinary people to borrow – whether that was to support their businesses or buy a new house. The cash shortage also happened to come at a time when food and fuel prices were soaring, putting the world's finances under even more pressure.

KNOW YOUR STUFF

The Credit Crunch... First the bad news

In January 2009, the UK was officially declared as being in recession. That means that the country had gone through two periods of three months each, where the amount of money it makes has gone down.

With less money in the system, many factories were forced to close and high street shops such as Woolworths went bust. This meant that thousands of people lost their jobs. In March 2009, a trade union reported that there were 10 people eligible for every job advertised at UK Job Centres.

...then some good news

Experts are hopeful that Britain's economy will be growing again by 2010. Gordon Brown and his Cabinet are now working with other countries to try and solve the money mess. In April 2009, 20 of the world's most important politicians gathered in London for a special meeting to discuss global issues. They agreed to make bank rules stricter so that the crisis doesn't happen again.

A CREDIT CRUNCHED CHRISTMAS

With less money available for treats, there was plenty of bah-humbug during Christmas 2008. Things got too much for the general public however when a couple of festive theme parks in England tried to charge top dollar for their very un-magical attractions. Lapland New Forest offered families an unforgettable Christmas experience. Instead disgruntled customers claimed that they'd been charged £25 a head to walk round a muddy field with very little to look at. Both Lapland New Forest and a similar park in the Midlands were quickly closed.

The credit crunch was such big news in 2008, the Queen even mentioned it in her annual Christmas Day speech. She said that although the season is usually a time for celebrating, 'this year it is a more sombre occasion for many.'

• PRESS PACK REPORT •

'Dad says the family is just trying to live through this.'

'Most children in my class have heard about the credit crunch, but they don't really understand what it means. I know, because my family has already been affected. My mum is a beautician and dad repairs windows and so far they are OK, but my gran and granddad have both recently lost their jobs. Gran worked as a nanny and Granddad repairs windows like my dad, but his company said they had to let some people go and he was one of them. My grandparents are both in their 50s so it is harder for them to find jobs than younger people and they couldn't pay their rent. Luckily they were able to come and live with us, but I still hear everyone talking about money a lot. I think it is a bad thing because everyone seems more stressed, my mum is working much longer hours and now she works on the weekend too. Before this all happened we used to have a lot of trips to places like Legoland, but now we don't go. I don't ask because I don't want to make Mum and Dad sad. We usually go on holiday in the summer to places like France and Spain too, but this year I don't think we can afford to. Mum wanted to go to Tunisia so I am putting any birthday money I get aside to help.'

Diana Savchuk, 10, North London.

TOP TIPS

Five easy ways to beat the cash crisis

- Throw toy swap parties with your friends

- Keep an eye out for discount vouchers for the best deals on days out or get your folks using websites such as www.moneysavingexpert.com

- Instead of ordering pizza, make your own. Pack a picnic instead of going to restaurants and takeaway shops.

- Get creative and customise old clothes before replacing them with new ones.

- Rent a DVD instead of taking a pricey trip to the cinema.

Rule Britannia

THE UPS AND DOWNS OF GORDON BROWN

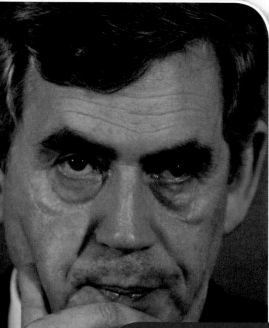

Gordon Brown

Since becoming Prime Minister of Great Britain, Gordon Brown has had to get through some challenging times. During 2008 some people didn't think that he was running the country very well. In July Labour suffered a massive election defeat in Scotland. Gordon's reputation took a further knock over scandals about the expenses that MPs claimed and reports that government workers had carelessly lost laptops containing important information. However – many people admire how Gordon has been dealing with the credit crunch, arguing that he's the only man who can get Britain out of the recession.

A vote from Harry Potter

In September 2008, *Harry Potter* writer J K Rowling made a grand political statement. She gave £1million to the Labour party because she believes that they have done a great deal to reduce child poverty. Gordon Brown, who is also her friend, said that he was thrilled to be supported by 'one of the world's greatest ever authors.'

When many of the world leaders came to London for the G20 summit meeting, J K Rowling entertained their wives by reading from her latest book *The Tales of Beedle the Bard*.

Prime Minister puzzle

How much do you know about Gordon Brown? Do this mini quiz to find out if you're a political hotshot when it comes to the PM!

1   **Where was Gordon Brown born?**
    a. *Bognor Regis*
    b. *Glasgow*
    c. *Liverpool*

2   **What was Gordon's last job before becoming PM?**
    a. *Chancellor of the Exchequer*
    b. *Home Secretary*
    c. *Leader of the House of Commons*

3   **Who is Gordon's favourite football team?**
    a. *Manchester United*
    b. *Accrington Stanley*
    c. *Raith Rovers*

4   **When he became PM, who did Gordon take over from?**
    a. *David Cameron*
    b. *Tony Blair*
    c. *Jack Straw*

5   **Where does Gordon and his family live?**
    a. *10 Downing Street*
    b. *The White House*
    c. *The Houses of Parliament*

Answers: 1a, 2a, 3c, 4b, 5a

KNOW YOUR STUFF

The UK has three main political parties – Labour, Conservatives and the Liberal Democrats. Gordon Brown leads Labour, the political party currently in power.

Since 2005, the Conservatives have been led by David Cameron. At the annual party conference in Birmingham, the leader described himself as a 'man with a plan' to win the next election and get Britain out of financial trouble. Nick Clegg has been leading the Liberal Democrats since December 2007. He is currently the youngest party leader in the UK.

In the House of Commons, there are other political groups that are voted for by the British public. These include national parties such as Wales' Plaid Cymru, the Scottish National Party and political groups from Northern Ireland.

For more information on what MPs do and how laws are made, visit the UK Parliament's website www.parliament.uk/about/guides.cfm and watch the mini slide shows.

Head to head! Opposition political leaders, Gordon Brown and David Cameron.

Make it happen!

KIDS IN PARLIAMENT

Newsround viewers have always believed that politics shouldn't be just left up to the grown-ups. During 2008, many of you took action to make sure that your voice was heard, whether that was by organising a protest about an issue that worried you, voting on your school council or joining a political party. Some Presspackers campaigned to help their local beauty spots – writing to their council, MPs and their local newspapers. Others stood for the UK Youth Parliament, a special organisation that helps young people bring about social change. In March 2009, MPs voted to allow members of the Youth Parliament to hold a meeting on the floor of the House of Commons. A session is planned for Summer 2009.

Seat of power. The Houses of Parliament and Big Ben sit on the bank of London's River Thames.

Three cheers for school councils!

There are more than 2,500 school councils in the UK already, with more being formed all the time. In some countries such as Ireland and Spain it is the law that every secondary school has one. In Great Britain it is not compulsory, but lots of kids feel that a council makes a positive difference to their life at school. Most school councils are made up of two representatives from each class. The representatives meet regularly to discuss problems and new proposals such as fundraising events, changes in school uniform or lunch menus. In larger schools there may be a separate council for each year group.

In protest

From protesting against post office closures to standing up for the environment, thousands of kids made banners and took to the streets in 2008.

'Save our school!' (January and February)
Hundreds of pupils campaigned about the closure of village schools. Around 100 schools in England, 29 in Wales and more in Northern Ireland were under threat as councils decided they were too small to run. Around 90 had already been closed in Scotland. Lots of kids in Shropshire took a day out to demonstrate.

'Put an end to knife crime' (July)
Hundreds of teenagers (pictured top right) staged a protest march through London to raise awareness of knife crime in the UK. The demonstration was led by the family and friends of a 16-year-old boy called Ben Kinsella who died after being stabbed in London earlier in July 2008. To read more about knife crime, turn to page 54.

'Improve education' (November)
Thousands of children in Germany went on strike from school because they were so unhappy about the standard of teaching in their country. Pupils argued that the school day was too long and there were too many kids in each class.

KNOW YOUR STUFF

More about the UKYP

What issues are important to you? Perhaps you think people should recycle more or you feel passionate about child poverty. If so, it might be time to stand for the UK Youth Parliament. Anybody between 11 and 18 can nominate themselves or vote for MYPs – young politicians that campaign about the issues that matter to them. Elections take place every year in every part of the UK.

There are over 500 elected Members and Deputy Members of the Youth Parliament.

Over 550,000 young people a year take part in elections.

Each Local Education Authority in England represents a UKYP constituency. The UKYP liaises with the Scottish Youth Parliament, Funky Dragon (Wales) and the Northern Ireland Youth Forum to ensure that the voices of all young people in the UK are represented at a national level.

The UKYP has links to regional Government Offices, Assemblies and Development Agencies to ensure young people's views are being heard and acted upon.

If you're interested in setting up a school council, check out www.schoolcouncils.org

Your politics

YOUR POLITICS Use this page to write your own political news stories and information.

You could also stick or clip, newspaper cuttings or pictures that you'd like to keep.

Kids and crime

KNIVES ON THE STREETS

Recently the news has been peppered with disturbing reports about violent crime amongst young people. Clocks had barely finished chiming in 2008 when the first two murders of the year occurred. In Leicester, Bradley Whitfield, 16, was stabbed in the neck. In Edmonton, 17-year-old Henry Bolombi was killed after getting off a night bus on his way home. In total there were 71 known victims of murder or manslaughter aged 10-19 in the UK in 2008, plus a further 18 in the first three months of 2009. This number includes victims of domestic violence and assault as well as gang-related deaths. The organisation No To Knives says that just under a third of all young people will carry an offensive weapon at some point during their teenage years. These reports make frightening reading, but it is important to remember that these crimes make the news because they are rare.

THE LAW ON KNIVES

In England, Northern Ireland and Wales, if you're under 18 you're not allowed to buy:

Any knife, blade or razor blade
Any axe
Any other article which has a blade or is sharply pointed
Anything which is made or adapted for use for causing injury to people.

In Scotland, you cannot buy any type of knife if you're under 16 years old.
There is a total ban for all ages on flick knives, butterfly knives and disguised knives – where the blade is hidden inside something like a belt buckle.

The laws about knives are complicated but across the UK and Republic of Ireland, it is generally against the law to carry a knife or an offensive weapon in a public place.

KNOW YOUR STUFF

Knife crime – THE FACTS

It's easy to believe knife crime is on the rise, but is it? Conflicting statistics from a variety of sources make it difficult to judge the truth. Firstly, it's important to remember The British Crime Survey does not currently record statistics for the under-16 age group – although in 2008 they announced this age bracket will be surveyed in future. Secondly, the media have been accused by some of fuelling 'public hysteria' with sensationalist reporting. In a recent study, Cambridge Professor David Spiegelhalter noted that while one front page headline in July 2008 screamed 'London's Murder Count Reaches 90', in reality this was an average number for that time of year. Despite the headlines, we are certainly not in the middle of a murder epidemic.

In the news

Too young to die

Two of the most high profile stories last year were the killings of teens Robert Knox in May 2008 and of Ben Kinsella a month later.

Aspiring actor Robert Knox, 18, had just finished filming his role as Marcus Belby in the film *Harry Potter and the Half Blood Prince* when he was attacked by Karl Bishop, 22, outside a bar in Sidcup. Robert was stabbed five times as he defended his brother Jamie. Tributes described him as a 'big teddy bear' who was 'loved by everyone'. Karl Bishop was jailed for twenty years in March 2009.

Ben Kinsella, 16, was the brother of former EastEnders actress Brooke Kinsella. The promising student was stabbed to death in Islington after being caught up in a fight that broke out at a party in a pub. He died in the arms of his friend Louis Robson, 16, son of actress Linda Robson.

Shortly after his death his parents discovered a story he'd written for an English class about a boy who was stabbed. Since his death his family have continued to campaign against knives. They are planning a Street Peace Live concert in 2009. Three young men are awaiting trial for murder.

Funeral and Thanksgiving Services
for the life of

Rob Knox

21st August 1989 – 24th May 2008
Wednesday 25th June 2008
Services led by Rev Neil Abbott,
Minister of Albany Park Baptist Church

KIDS IN GANGS

On 12 February 2009, the Centre for Social Justice published a report called Dying to Belong: a review of street gangs in Britain. The report suggested as many as 6% of ten to 16-year-olds are members of gangs. Some gang members it alleged, are even as young as eight years old. Iain Duncan Smith, who used to lead the Conservative Party and set up the CSJ, spent 14 months working on the report and finding out why children join gangs. He said that 'half the teenagers murdered in London last year were the victims of gang crime. That should bring home the brutal truth that street gangs are nasty.' The report stated that most young gang members have experienced family problems and are no longer going to school. They are usually from very deprived, high-crime neighbourhoods and because they feel alienated by society, turn to gang culture as a way to 'belong' and to gain 'respect'.

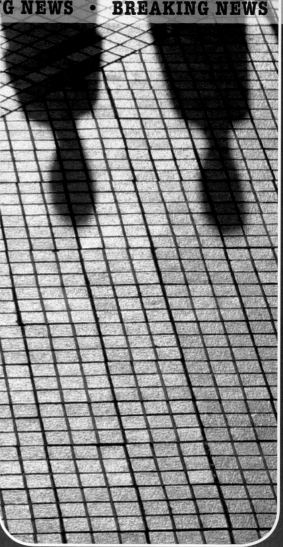

The wider effects

Although the number of people actually involved in gangs is quite small, their actions and behaviour affect a much wider section of society. Gangs are often involved in selling drugs, carrying out robberies, assaults or anti-social behaviour; all of which upset or hurt others.

The rise in the number of young people carrying knives might also be due to a growing fear of gangs. In a recent Crimestoppers survey, 46% of under 16s questioned said they were frightened of teenage gangs. Most young people who admit carrying a knife claim to do so for protection rather than to threaten or injure someone.

PAGE 126 If you worry about gangs and knife crime, turn to page 126 to find out how to

What's the way forward?

The Dying to Belong report says that all gang members should be made to stop the violence or go to jail. Every time they break the law, even if it's just by dropping litter, they should be prosecuted. Other tough ideas include having Gang Prevention Zones in areas where there is a lot of crime. In these places police and other experts would work closely together to break up gangs and to stop new ones being set up. But the report also says that trust needs to be built between the police and young people to stop a new generation being lost to gangs. In the future it argues that adults need to look at the 'needs' rather than the 'deeds' of those involved; what might be missing in these kids' lives and how things can be changed so that they can start again.

SHOCKING FACTS

Drink and drugs

Youth crime is often blamed on the problems of under-age drinking and drug taking. Here are some statistics about alcohol and drugs from a recent survey carried out for the NHS in schools during 2007.

- The proportion of 11 to 15-year-olds across England who have never drunk alcohol has risen from 39% in 2003 to 46% in 2007.

- Over half of 11 to 15-year-olds had drunk at least one alcohol drink in their lifetime. This increases with age from 20% of 11-year-olds to 81% of 15-year-olds.

- Of those who drank, the average weekly consumption has more than doubled since 1990 from 5.3 units a week to 11.4 units per week in 2006.

- Boys tend to drink more than girls. Boys who drank in the last week drank more units of alcohol (13.1 units) than girls who drank in the last week (12.4 units).

- A comparative European study of drinking among 15 to 24-year-olds showed that UK figures for alcohol consumption were some of the highest in Europe.

cope with this type of news.

BROWN'S CRACKDOWN

It's easy to feel powerless in the face of issues like knife crime. The important thing is to try and understand what's really being done and then find out what you can do to help.

Parents, the police and the government are actually doing a number of things to fight back against violence amongst young people. Operation Blunt II ran from May to June 2008. During the Operation the Metropolitan Police carried out nearly 27,000 searches in London. Over 1,200 people were arrested for offences connected to knives and 500 knives were seized. In the summer of 2008 The Home Office also announced its Youth Crime Action Plan detailing a new approach to knife crime. Its key measures included:

- Doubling maximum sentences for possession of a knife in public without good reason, from two to four years.

- Providing 100 portable knife arches and 400 search wands, with more planned over the next three years.

- Introducing a national three year £3 million ad campaign to challenge the 'glamour', fear and peer pressure that motivate young people to carry knives.

- Giving police greater powers to prosecute anyone found carrying a knife. This applies to everyone aged 16 and over – and applies to those under 16 on a second offence.

- Definite custodial sentences for those caught using a knife and increased likelihood of custodial sentence for knife carrying.

Anti-social behaviour

Anti-social behaviour means intimidating or threatening activity that scares you or damages your quality of life.

Examples include rowdy behaviour, vandalism, graffiti, tipping rubbish or setting off fireworks. Anyone doing these things could be fined, have to sign an Acceptable Behaviour Contract or even be issued with an ASBO.

Anti-social behaviour orders (ASBOs) are court orders issued by local authorities or the police against trouble-makers, which last a minimum of two years and forbid the person to behave badly, hang out with particular groups or visit certain areas.

There has been a lot of discussion in the press about ASBOs and whether they work. Many think they don't because teenagers see them as 'badges of honour'. The police can't enforce them properly and councils don't like issuing them because of the paperwork involved. Some newspapers have chosen to 'name and shame' children with ASBOs who continue to cause disruption, something the Youth Justice Board believes is wrong.

There have also been bizarre cases of ASBOs issued like one preventing a young boy from playing football, and another telling an 87-year-old grandfather to stop being sarcastic.

KNOW YOUR STUFF

Staying safe

Mark Cooper from No To Knives says:

- Speak to an adult if you're scared or being bullied and avoid areas you know to be dodgy.

- Never, ever go near someone holding a knife.

- Distance is your greatest protection if someone pulls a knife on you. Get as far away as you can.

- Run away, walk in a shop or a place where there are people and make lots of noise to draw attention to yourself.

- Never carry a knife as protection – they are designed to attack not defend so they will not stop you from getting hurt. Instead they increase your risk of escalating a situation and getting injured.

In the news

Police announce anonymous text scheme

In January 2009 the police announced they were trialling a new scheme in ten areas around England and Wales to get kids to report by text anyone they know who is carrying a knife. Young people can now send an anonymous text message to a special Crimestoppers number, 88551, so no-one will know that they've sent it. The messages are passed over to police officers. Richard Spedding from Lancashire police said he hopes the scheme will get more kids to help stop knife crime.

Do kids today get a bad press?

Amidst the perpetual doom and gloom reports about hoodies and the decline of today's young people, there are real, heartwarming and inspiring stories proving that children are capable of amazing acts of kindness and courage:

Seven-year-old William John from Swansea, who cares for his mum Wendy who has Multiple Sclerosis, and Courtney Taylor, 10, who led her mum to safety when their house caught fire, both won Children of Courage Awards in 2008. The Daily Mirror Pride of Britain 2008 Awards honoured Liam Fairhurst, 13, from Soham who despite having cancer raised £150,000 to help other sick kids and Jaden Ashton, 6, who saved his mum by calling 999 and tending to her when she fell into a diabetic coma.

In March 2009, John Clark and Andrew Kellock from Inverness were praised for steering a school minibus to safety when the teacher who was driving them home from a rugby match fell unconscious at the wheel.

THE AGE OF SCAMS

These days access to technology means people who want to cheat us out of our personal information and our money can target us as never before – via mobile phone or computer. One scam which hit the headlines in 2009 involved website con-artists issuing fake tickets to concerts such as Girls Aloud and festivals like V and Glastonbury. Every year 30,000 people book concert tickets online, only to find they never arrive or are invalid. In another scam in March 2009 a group of teens from Wiltshire had their dream to compete in a Hollywood Dance Contest shattered when the administrator from their dance school ran off with £27,000 they had saved for flights and accommodation.

Common cons to avoid

The wannabe scam

Some people set up fake modelling or casting agencies and persuade girls and boys to pay lots of money to have a portfolio of photos taken or to 'audition' for a role that doesn't exist. People pretending to be film producers or model scouts advertise on castings websites or target individuals via social networking sites. For more information on scams and how to find reputable model agencies visit www.albamodel.info

The charity scam

A leaflet comes through your letter box saying that if you leave out your old clothes and toys in the bag provided, they'll be collected and the money given to charity. In fact many of these are not charities, but businesses who sell your possessions for profit.

The texting scam

This popular scam sends out text messages urging you to call back on what is actually a really expensive rate phone line. Scammers often send the same message up to 40 times a day to hundreds of numbers, waiting for its targets to get fed up and call back.

KNOW YOUR STUFF

FAB OR FAKE?

If you've saved up for something, the last thing you want is to find out that it's a poor quality fake. Counterfeit goods are big business, but they bring misery as they are often badly made and can break. How can you check what you're buying is the real deal? As a rule, if something which is usually a lot of money is being offered to you at a knockdown price, the chances are that it's not what it appears to be.

Toys

Fake toys often break easily, which means they pose a choking risk for younger children. Look for the BSI Kite, CE and Lion quality marks which show the toy has passed safety tests. Also make sure they are given to you in sealed packaging.

Trainers

Because of their popularity big names like Nike and Adidas are especially prone to sub-standard copy-cats. Before buying, check on the official website for the colours that a style comes in and the way the brand name is shown. Counterfeits often have the name glued rather than stitched on and are available in a wider range of shades. The stitching is also a give away – it should be tight and even.

Computer games

These are easy to copy so you need to be suspicious if someone has several disks of a great new game that's difficult to find in the big stores.

DVDs or CDs

These might have sound but no picture, picture but no sound, not work at all, or even have been filmed from a camcorder in a cinema so that you can see people's heads in front of the screen. Beware of those without security holograms or with badly printed labels.

Young entrepreneurs

Some kids not only save their pocket money, but use it to make more. Meet some of Britain's youngest and smartest entrepreneurs...

Matt Lovett, 17, set up his first business aged 12, buying cheap sweets in bulk and selling them to classmates. He now runs his own marketing company WOW Media – a collection of cashback websites which give subscribers discounts and special offers when they buy items from certain retailers. Company turnover is reportedly £25,000 a month and he recently won the teen category of the 2009 Make Your Mark Enterprising Young Brits Awards.

Did you know?

A survey by RBS showed that the average entrepreneur is a youngest child, does a paper round and is competitive at sport.

Louis Barnett (pictured right), 17, transformed his hobby into a business aged just 12, after spotting a gap in the market for making not only his products but the packaging out of chocolate. He became the youngest supplier ever of Waitrose and Sainsbury's and his current range includes Bite Back Bars, where a percentage of the profit goes to fund wildlife protection charities. Visit www.chokolit.co.uk

Eighteen-year-old entrepreneur Jellyellie was 13 when she created the hit technology website bluejackQ.com which was featured in international media. At 15, she signed a publishing deal for her first book, *How Teenagers Think*, an insider's guide for parents about teenagers. She currently speaks at conferences worldwide and runs a youth insight agency giving companies invaluable access to today's young people.

In the news

Make your Mark with a Tenner

February 2009 saw the re-launch of a competition designed to motivate budding entrepreneurs. Backing came from millionaire businessman Peter Jones, star of Dragon's Den and the couple who founded Bebo. The Make Your Mark team loaned £10 to 20,000 young people and challenged them to make as much profit as they could. Individuals were able to take on the challenge alone, or work with friends and pool their £10 notes. The competition last ran in 2007 and was won by Fazila Dadabhoy from Walthamstow School for Girls in London. She made £410 from making and selling doughnuts and donated her profit to charity. Five students from Holmer Green Senior School in High Wycombe, made £1,000 by organizing activities and competitions – their money helped rebuild a school in Kenya. Michael and Xochi Birch, of Bebo, said 'Children and young people are naturally innovative and creative. Make Your Mark with a Tenner allows them to channel that natural ability while focusing on a very noble goal.'

COOL FACTS

Do you save or spend?

In August 2008 the Halifax Building Society published the results of research into children's pocket money. This is what they found:

- The average amount of pocket money received in 2008 was £6.13 a week. This has dropped from 2007 when the average was £8.01.

- Children in London and Scotland receive the most pocket money, £8.47 and £8.20 respectively. Those in the East Midlands and the South West receive just £4.46 and £4.58 respectively.

- Three in ten children save some of their pocket money each week. More than a quarter of children do not save any of their pocket money and most tend to frequently ask for additions to their allowance as gifts.

SOCIAL NETWORKING EXPLODES

Social networking sites like Facebook, Twitter and Bebo seem here to stay, and in April 2008 Media Watchdog Ofcom proved their popularity among the pre-teen population with the results of a survey on children and social networking. They showed that although most sites set a minimum age of 13, none actively enforce the limit and in fact more than a quarter of eight to 11-year-olds who are online in the UK have a profile on a social network.

Using the Net for school – research or cheating?

Do you use the net for schoolwork? If so you might need to ask yourself if what you're doing is really research. Copying someone else's work from the net and pretending it's your own – rather than quoting who said it – is called internet plagiarism or academic dishonesty. It is seen as a very serious offence and can result in you failing a grade on a particular assignment or for the entire course. From 2009, GCSE coursework will be scrapped in nine academic subjects. Instead pupils will complete projects in the classroom under supervision.

GET WEB WISE

Whether you are using a networking site or just chatting on a forum or in a chatroom, you might be putting personal information online. Once the info's out there you may not be able to control what happens to it. This could pose a risk to your privacy or your personal safety, so think before giving out information. Unless you have an adult's permission NEVER reveal:

- Your real name
- Your home, school or email address
- Your phone number
- A photo of yourself
- Your parents' credit card details

ALWAYS tell a responsible adult if you receive rude or unpleasant emails or a chat room message that makes you feel uncomfortable.

A new breed of bully

Cyber bullying is when someone intimidates another person by sending horrible or threatening messages by phone or computer. Victims might also find personal information or photos posted somewhere without their knowledge. In June 2008, Britain was rocked by the news that 13-year-old Sam Leeson killed himself after being bullied on Bebo because of his taste in music and clothes. According to charity Beatbullying (www.beatbullying.org) a third of 11 to 18-year-olds now say they've suffered from cyber bullying.

In February 2009, the government announced it's backing for a scheme offering victims help. A new social networking website has been set up called www.cybermentors.org.uk. Victims of cyberbullying can go online and speak to others who've been through the same experiences.

Dot.coms

Be wary of other emails that might pop into your inbox!

Phishing

When this happens, someone sends you an email which seems as if it's from a reputable organisation or company that you know and deal with. Social networking sites or banks and building societies are often copied in this way. The email will say that you need to confirm your details, but when you send your info through, the scammers will steal your money or your identity. What to do: never give out your details without first showing an adult the email you've received.

Downloads

A certain percentage contain viruses that can harm your computer, steal your personal data and end up in identity theft. You might be on a site but receive a message saying that you have to download a plug-in in order to continue. Later you will discover that your computer has a virus, by which time fraudsters might already be pretending to be you.
What to do: ask an adult to put a good firewall up plus a virus detector to protect your computer. Don't download things without checking with an adult first.

Don't respond to nasty texts or emails; Save upsetting messages to show adults.

Your citizenship

YOUR CITIZENSHIP Use this page to write your own citizenship news stories and information.

School news

TRUANCY ON THE RISE

Government statistics released in February this year showed that although the total authorized absence rate fell to its lowest ever level, at the same time the unauthorized absence rate rose to the highest level on record, with around 63,000 children away from class during any given school session, or half-day.

More than 233,000 schoolchildren in England are "persistent absentees" – missing at least one day of school every week.

And while absences among secondary pupils fell, increasing numbers of primary school children skipped school or arrived late, with more than 18,600 missing a school session each day through truancy, illness and other reasons.

With truancy on the rise, the government needs to look at the root causes

In the news
The SATS debate

In October 2008 Ed Balls, the Secretary for Schools, announced that SATS exams for 14-year-olds were to be scrapped immediately.

The move came after years of mounting criticism from teachers and parents who said that such testing at an early age puts too much pressure on children.

With the decision universally welcomed, there is now speculation about the future of SATS for younger pupils, particularly as the latest league tables showed around 150,000 pupils failed to achieve the government's expected standards in English and Maths. Mick Brookes, general secretary for the National Association of Head Teachers (NAHT) expressed concern saying: "England's 10/11 year olds will be the only children in the UK to be put under this pressure. If it is right to end the regime in Key Stage 1 and Key Stage 3 and get rid of all SATS in Scotland, Wales and Northern Ireland, surely the same logic applies to English children at Key Stage 2." Ed Ball announced in May 2009, that science SATs are to be abolished in favour of teacher assessment in the near future.

• PRESS PACK REPORT •

Jake Schepuck is 12 and lives in Middlesex. In June 2008 he was awarded the Anti-bullying Award at the annual Diana Awards which recognise children who have given something back to their community.

'Last year I was in Year 6 at Suffolks Primary School, Enfield. The school has been operating an anti-bullying mentoring scheme for about three years and I got involved in Year 5. You put your name in a box if you're interested in taking part and then they give you a timetable to let you know which days you'll be on duty and in what part of the school. At any playtime or lunchtime there are always two mentors in the playground with the nursery kids and Year 1s and another two mentors on the field with Years 2 – 6. As a mentor your job is to keep an eye out for signs of bullying and fighting. Having mentors around means it's less likely to happen but there were a few times when we had to step in. I once caught two Year 3 kids in a bush trying to steal a boy's calculator,

Bullying can ruin a child's life.

so I gave the teacher the names and they were dealt with by the Head. I also helped break up a fight between two Year 4s by calming things down while the other mentor fetched a teacher.

When I got my award I felt really proud. We went up to London for the ceremony and had lunch and Esther Rantzen presented us with our badges. Afterwards the teachers took us on the London Eye.

I think mentoring is a great idea as bullying can ruin kids' lives. Being a mentor is a nice feeling as you meet and help other kids you might not have mixed with otherwise. Now I'm in senior school where they don't have mentors but they do have a zero tolerance policy and there are CCTV cameras and more teachers on the field, so you still feel safe.'

For more information about the Diana Awards visit
www.diana-award.org.uk

BULLYING

Bullying remains a key priority for the government and for the Department for Children, Schools and Families (DCSF) has made clear that no form of bullying should be tolerated. In 2007 Safe to Learn: embedding anti-bullying work in schools, was launched as guidance for schools. They now have to have measures in place to encourage good behaviour and respect for others, and to prevent all forms of bullying. Schools can also sign up to the Anti-bullying Charter to show their commitment to tackling bullying.

The burning issues

ARE YOU SAFE IN SCHOOLS?

There have been several school massacres in America, but in September 2008, Europe hit the headlines when Matti Saari, 22, killed nine fellow students and a teacher before shooting himself at a school in Kauhajoki, Finland. In March 2009, 17-year-old Tim Kretschmer, from Winnenden, Germany, fatally shot nine pupils and three teachers from his former school.

Such events have prompted debate about security in UK schools. So how safe are we? The good news is that these events remain rare, the only incidence of this happening in the UK was in 1996 at Dunblane, and after that the government outlawed handguns completely. The government continues to work towards ensuring our safety in school and in 2007 launched the Secured Environment initiative. This means schools now have to show an understanding of what security means and implement measures such as keeping school gates bolted and having one main entrance in use to make monitoring of strangers much easier.

Philosophy for kids debate

In autumn 2008 it was announced that some Primary schools are trialling philosophy lessons for children in Year 3.

Some adults think children of 7 and 8 are too young to understand such difficult concepts and should instead be concentrating on learning to read and write well. Others argue that it teaches lateral thinking and broadens the mind. Philosophy involves questioning the way we think and often there is no right or wrong answer... Below is one of the questions you might come across as a Year 3 philosophy pupil. What do you think?

The frog and the scorpion - The scorpion had seen members of his family on the other side of a river and wanted the frog to ferry him across. The frog was reluctant. "You'll sting me with your deadly tail." The scorpion promised he would not, but half-way across he stung the frog. "That's what I do," he told the frog as both slid to their watery grave.

Who is to blame? It's a matter of opinion. The scorpion stung the frog and caused them both to die. The frog knew that the scorpion would probably sting him and had the choice not to carry him. Also, the scorpion couldn't help his nature.

WORLD'S BIGGEST LESSON

In April 2008 teachers, children, parents and campaigners united around the globe to set a Guinness World Record for the world's biggest lesson. In total 8.8 million people took part in the scheme, organized by the Global Campaign for Education, which aims to ensure a quality education for everyone. The lesson focused on the fact that 72 million children around the world are not educated. 57% of girls are excluded from having an education, often because their parents think daughters should help at home and then be married off. Half the children who don't go to school are in war zones and some of their schools have been bombed.

FUN QUIZ ALL ABOUT SCHOOL

1 **What percentage of pupils gained pass grades A* - C for GCSEs in 2008?**
a. 81.3%   b. 42.1%   c. 65.7%

2 **What percentage of primary school children have school dinners?**
a. 42%   b. 30%   c. 54%

3 **How many schools are there in total in the UK?**
a. 17, 920   b. 25, 335   c. 34, 333

4 **A school in Gateshead recently adopted some animals to help pupils with lessons, were they...**
a. Racing pigeons?
b. Hamsters?
c. Monkeys at the local zoo?

5 **A June 2008 study revealed that adults struggle to understand Primary School level teaching. Only one-in-20 correctly answered 10 questions taken from primary school syllabuses. What was the thing most of them got wrong?**
a. They thought Shakespeare's first name was Walter.
b. They didn't know the capital of Sweden.
c. They couldn't spell the world skilful.

6 **Why did Watercliffe Meadow school recently make the news?**
a. It got the highest SATS pass rate in the country
b. The meadows behind it flooded.
c. The headmistress wanted it to be called 'a place of learning' rather than a 'school'.

7 **In June 2008 a male supply teacher was asked to leave a school in Sudbury Suffolk after he:**
a. Fell asleep in class.
b. Took his shirt off – having told the class that if they misbehaved they'd have to look at his body.
c. Helped the class to cheat in their mock GCSE exams.

8 **According to the Sunday Times Parent Power Schools tables, the top state Primary school in 2008 was:**
a. St Anne's C of E VC Primary, Bakewell, Derbyshire.
b. Spinfield School, Marlow, Buckinghamshire.
c. South Farnham School, Farnham, Surrey.

9 **What did Greenwood School in Nottingham do, which infuriated parents last year?**
a. They cancelled the school nativity play because it clashed with the Muslim festival of Eid.
b. They started searching packed lunch boxes to check pupils were eating healthily.
c. They began excluding pupils who didn't have clean, ironed school uniform.

10 **What did thousands of schools in Scotland ban last year?**
a. Mobile phones.
b. Pupils from making Father's Day cards.
c. Fake tans.

Answers:1c; 2a; 3b; 4a; 5c (The study revealed that most adults were stumped by the correct spelling of a basic word - skilful - with only 23% getting it right); 6c (the word 'school' was said to have 'negative connotations'); 7b; 8c (St Anne's came 20th and Spinfield was 10th); 9a; 10b (they said that this was to avoid upsetting pupils from single-mother families – however a school in Cheshire did ban fake tans.).

Your school news

You could also stick or clip, newspaper cuttings or pictures that you'd like to keep.

73

Ore Oduba

1 Describe your path into presenting Newsround?
I've wanted to be a presenter since my last couple of years at secondary school so, as well as being heavily involved in sport at university, I learned about some areas of journalism in my degree, and I took advantage of the tremendous media centre we had there. I was an editor for our magazine, had my own radio show and produced and presented lots of our TV shows. I put a showreel together and was ecstatic to be able to audition for the job at Newsround. The rest, I guess, is history… (does everybody else say that??)

2 Which of the past year's news stories particularly struck a chord with you?
The Beijing Olympics in 2008 I'd say. It was the first massive story I experienced at Newsround – it all kicked off only a couple of weeks after I started. I am a real sports fan and of course the Olympics showcase the best sportspeople in the world, so I was already massively interested and excited about it. With Sonali reporting from China, we were able to do lots of live link ups and it felt great that Newsround was there to witness the best Team GB performance for a hundred years.

3 What's the most exciting thing about your job?
Personally I just love the live aspect of television and with news, of course, presenting from the studio has to be live so I really enjoy that. When we have a live link up in the studio with someone from the red carpet of an awards ceremony or from another country, for example, it's very exciting. You hopefully get a good idea of the atmosphere of wherever the link up is coming from. Hopefully in the future I'll be able to report from lots of places live for Newsround too.

4 Are there any downsides to being a news reporter/presenter?
There aren't many because I'm doing a job I really enjoy, but it can sometimes be quite full on. Some days can be long which means you don't get to see your friends or do other things as much as you might want. Believe me, though, I don't often have much to complain about!

5 Have you had any on-screen disasters so far?
Fortunately there really haven't been many (fingers crossed, touch wood!) Once we weren't able to play a report in a bulletin which meant I had to talk about it instead for about a minute, but it was about football, so it didn't go too badly! The technical team at NR are great so I trust them not to make me look silly – they leave that up to me!

Ore preparing for Newsround.

Ore reporting out and about for Newsround.

6 **Was there anything you found difficult to cover and how do you cope with negative or distressing stories?**
It can be quite difficult to report about negative stories like the bombings in Mumbai or even the riots in Greece at the end of 2008. It's the case with every story, but we have to be especially careful with stories like that to make sure we've got the facts right like who was involved and why etc. They can be upsetting for viewers so we have to be sensitive to that and make sure we cover them in the right way.

7 **What do you do in a typical day?**
My days at NR can be really different, varying from interviewing someone, reporting from somewhere around the country or filming for Sportsround. On a typical day, though, once I've come in, I chat with our producer and assistant producer about the story we'll be covering. If we need to do an interview or film something we'll try to get that done as soon as possible before coming back to edit it all together. I then will present the bulletin at 3.55pm before preparing for the 5.05pm programme on BBC1. After the programme meeting with the rest of the NR team there's one more bulletin at 6.25pm to present and then it's home time.

8 **What has been the biggest news story you've ever covered and what made it so important?**
It's got to be Barack Obama's inauguration as US President. It was a story the whole world was tuned in to watch and something we'd been preparing for a while. Adam was live in Washington and we were on air the moment Obama was sworn in. We even managed to record that very piece of history and put it on the programme. I was quite nervous because it was such a huge story and I really wanted us to be able to do it justice... I don't think we could have done it any better – quality!

Controversial science

A tray containing stem cells, at the Sao Paulo University Human Genome Research Centre in Sao Paulo.

ATTACK OF THE CLONES

Laboratories that clone plants and animals have divided scientists and the public for years. When cloning happens, it means that a new life has been made out of another living thing. The clone is made using the genes of the first plant or animal, and so both have the same DNA. In August 2008 experts in South Korea claimed to have cloned the first pet. When Bernann McKinney from the US found out that her dog Booger was dying, she paid scientists to use some of his skin cells to make a new version of him. The cells were implanted into another dog that gave birth to five puppies, all the spitting image of Booger. The animal charity RSPCA isn't so impressed. They warn that a clone is never exactly the same as its parent, pointing out that there are already thousands of animals around that are in desperate of a good home.

RETURN OF THE FROZEN MICE

Japanese scientists caused a stir in November 2008 when they cultivated clones from mice that had been dead for 16 years.

The animals had been frozen in a special lab so that their genes were preserved. Cloning dead animals is a huge breakthrough – using this knowledge scientists hope to one day clone extinct species. Could there even be a real Jurassic Park where prehistoric creatures are given the chance to walk the Earth once more?

KNOW YOUR STUFF

Cloning can be confusing. Here's a quick guide to how it works...

Cloning happens in nature all the time. Plants that grow from cuttings are a great example. Some types of grass can also spore whole new plants by sending out shoots. Identical twins are naturally-occurring clones, although they do have different genes from their parents.

Scientists have been trying to clone plants and animals for decades. Their first great success came in 1997 when Dolly the Sheep became the first cloned mammal. It took 276 tries to make her.

Since Dolly, cows, pigs, dogs, monkeys, mice, cats and horses have all been cloned. In 2005, British scientists announced that they had successfully cloned the country's first human embryo. It was made illegal to clone embryos to make babies in 2001, so scientists only use the cells to help them research disease.

Some people argue that cloning is wrong because it isn't natural. The vast majority of the attempts at cloning don't work, but other experts feel that this area of science is still important. They argue that cloning could help grow new organs for sick people or find cures for illnesses like diabetes.

CLONED PEOPLE NEXT?

In April 2008 scientists unveiled a method that they said would make it possible to create a cloned child. The technique reprogrammes skin cells so that they go back to how they were as an embryo. A few months earlier, a scientist called Dr Samuel Wood also announced that he had successfully cloned himself. The embryos that he created were smaller than a pinhead and only survived for five days.

This major milestone has got lots of people worried. Many are concerned that this knowledge could enable labs to produce 'designer babies'. Although the scientists have no plans to use the technology in this way, there are fears that the technique might fall into the wrong hands. New laws are being reviewed and introduced all the time to try and keep up with progress in cloning.

There are tons of facts, fascinating questions and experiments to try out.

SUPER FOODS?

Feeding the world is getting harder and harder. In March 2009 a top US scientist claimed that Earth had 'exceeded its limits'. The world already has a population of 6.8 billion hungry mouths, each needing food and shelter. The US Census Bureau now predicts that by 2040 there could 9 billion of us living on the planet. Nina Fedoroff is an advisor to the American Secretary of State, Hillary Clinton. She believes that the world needs to manage its land better and turn to science in order to avoid food shortages. Some agree that Genetically Modified Foods could be at least part of the solution. GM foods are seeds that have been artificially developed by scientists in labs so that they grow stronger than normal crops. GM plants such as barley can be engineered so that it is more drought resistant or longer lasting than its natural form. Many people are against tampering with nature in this way. As time goes on however, GM foods may provide an option that world leaders can't afford to ignore.

• PRESS PACK REPORT •

'The vegetables that we grow at home taste much better than the shop bought ones.'

'My Mum and Dad are really concerned about GM food and they have been buying organic meat and vegetables for years. When our food bills started going up they got an allotment. We still buy organic meat, but now we grow all our own vegetables. I really like the fact that I've watched how and when the plants grow. When you go to the supermarket you can get anything at any time and things stay on the shelves for ages. That's because they put all sorts of chemicals in them to make them grow faster or last longer. That's really worrying. I don't like putting things in my body like that so I'm glad we're doing it our way.'

Hannah Snee, 11, Newmarket, Suffolk.

KNOW YOUR STUFF

Where do you stand on GM Foods?

Some EU countries have placed a ban on growing GM foods on their lands. In April 2009, Germany joined this group by banning the production of GM maize on its soil. The government claims that the maize is a danger to the environment, but what do you think?

The case for...

Avoid starvation
Many scientists believe that the use of GM technology is the only way we can harvest enough crops to feed the world's growing population.

Cheaper food
If crops were more plentiful, the price of food would come down. This would be a life-changing step forward for poorer countries and the developing world.

Stronger, tastier crops
GM foods can be bred to fight off pests and poor weather conditions. This means that fewer crops would be spoilt by weeds, drought or flood.

... and against

Bad for your health?
Research has shown that rats that are fed GM food don't always grow properly. Because this science is new, no one has been able to run proper safety tests on GM crops.

Unleash new diseases
Playing with nature could create new super-bugs and diseases with the power to cause major damage to our existing crops.

Anti-nature
Mixing up different species might lead to unexpected side effects. There is also a risk that GM foods could upset the delicate ecosystems that keep the natural world allive.

Nearly all groceries that use GM foods have got a clear label on the packaging. That way you can decide whether you want to eat them or not.

Amazing medicine

NEW HOPE FOR ALLERGY KIDS

Living with a peanut allergy can be tough. One in every fifty children has a strong reaction if they eat or even touch nuts. Medical research in 2008 brought some good news however. A group of kids with a peanut allergy had their condition cured after doctors at Cambridge's Addenbrooke's Hospital tried a new treatment on them. The four children were given a small amount of peanut flour to eat every day. Over the course of six months, doctors slowly increased the amount of flour that they ate. By the end of the trial all the children had become less sensitive to peanuts, and were even able to eat five a day without any reaction. The research was carefully carried out by experts, so please don't try this yourself if you have a nut allergy. The treatment isn't a permanent cure, but if the kids carry on eating nuts every day their tolerance is likely to continue.

ALLERGIES ON THE UP?

The number of people suffering from more than one allergy in the UK has doubled according to doctors. Children are likely to have a handful of allergies, ranging from hay fever to asthma. Expert Dr Adam Fox told Sonali that 'people who get allergies have been unlucky enough to get a tendency to have allergies from their parents, and if you've got that tendency then you're more likely to get more than one allergy.'

If you think you might be intolerant to something, ask your mum or dad to take you to the doctor for a proper test. As soon as you confirm the allergy, you can start treating its symptoms.

In the news

Brilliant Breakthroughs
New medical treatments take years to test and millions of pounds to fund. Here are three of the most exciting recent breakthroughs:

Surgery without the scars
Leading doctors are now experimenting with a new type of surgery that doesn't involve cutting patients open. 'Natural orifice' surgery is performed by entering the body through existing openings such as the mouth or colon. Surgeons at the University of Diego successfully removed a woman's appendix in this way in March 2008.

No more ringing in the ears
In March 2009, Australian experts announced that they are getting closer to finding a cure to tinnitus - a terrible ringing in the ears that won't go away. The doctors carried out tests on guinea pigs that suggested that the ringing is caused by uncontrolled nerve activity in the brain.

New blood test for Down's syndrome
A new test might be able to offer pregnant mums an easier way of finding out if their unborn child has Down's syndrome. A simple blood test taken from the mother would allow scientists to look at the baby's DNA through a microscope and then spot any genetic conditions.

PAXMAN DONATES HIS BRAIN TO SCIENCE

Heavyweight news journalist Jeremy Paxman made a bold pledge in April 2009.

He offered to leave his brain after his death so that it can be used by scientists researching Parkinson's disease. Parkinson's is a serious condition that limits movement and speech, as well as causing limbs to shake or go rigid.

Jeremy's promise was announced as part of a special campaign to find more brain donors. Researchers into Parkinson's say that their work is being held back because of a shortage of brain tissue to study. Only 1,000 people are on the Parkinson's Disease Society's Brain Donor Register. The charity have teamed up with Jeremy and other famous people to try and persuade as many people as possible to donate their brain for the benefit of others in the future.

The 'Final Frontier'

To track where the ISS is right now, log on to http://spaceflight.nasa.gov/realdata/tracking/

HAPPY BIRTHDAY!

On November 2008 the International Space Station (ISS) turned 10, although it is still a long way off being finished. During the years that the ISS has been orbiting the Earth, US space agency NASA have been working towards making it a permanent presence in the skies. Fourteen countries have pledged their time, knowledge and an awful lot of money to the ISS. Space shuttles regularly fly up to the ISS, bringing equipment and astronauts to carry out on the complex renovations. The improvements mean that the number of astronauts working and conducting experiments aboard ISS at any one time can increase from three to six. The work needs to be completed by 2010, because that's when NASA's fleet of space shuttles are being retired.

In the news

Satellite SOS!

On February 10th 2009 news channels reported the biggest known space crash in history. An American spacecraft collided with a Russian satellite about 800 kilometres above Siberia. The US Iridium spacecraft was used for satellite telephone calls, but the Russian machinery hadn't been working since 2007. There are about 6,000 satellites orbiting the Earth, but a crash like this is very unusual.

In January 2008, the US government decided to shoot down a spy satellite that was plummeting to Earth. Many satellites fall to the ground without causing any problems, but experts were worried that this one had a toxic fuel tank. The out-of-control satellite was hit by a missile as it returned to the Earth's atmosphere above the ocean near Hawaii.

KNOW YOUR STUFF

Radical renovations

The last few months have been busy on the International Space Station.

Science lab from Europe

The space shuttle Atlantis had a successful 13-day trip to space in February 2008. Seven astronauts went up to the ISS to install Europe's first science laboratory. The £1 billion lab has been christened Columbus.

Unmanned visitor

An unmanned space truck docked with the ISS in April 2008. The Automated Transfer Vehicle (ATV) is a giant spacecraft that delivered about five tonnes of food, water, air, fuel and equipment.

Special delivery

It was the space shuttle Discovery's turn for a mission in June 2008. The Discovery delivered an enormous Japanese science lab to the space station, plus a pump to fix a broken toilet.

Changing rooms

In November 2008 the space shuttle Endeavour docked on the ISS, ready to give the crew's living area a makeover. During the 15-day mission the astronauts fitted new ovens, a fridge and an extra bathroom. They also started building another bedroom.

New solar panels

In March 2009 astronauts completed the first of three space walks to fit extra solar wings to the ISS. The solar panels will give the station a big power boost. The brightness of the panels may even make the ISS easier to spot from Earth.

A satellite view of the space shuttle Atlantis.

An artist's impression of a supernova black hole.

NEW SPACESHIP FOR NASA

In March 2009 the USA unveiled a model of Orion – the brand new spaceship that will take over after the Space Shuttle has been retired. The Orion is a massive machine, based on designs of the original Apollo spacecraft that first took Americans to the Moon. Experts hope to stage the first launch to the ISS in 2015 before travelling to the Moon and on to Mars.

Great gadgets

Budding inventors and scientists from all over the UK showed what bright young minds can come up with at the Big Bang Fair 2009 at London's QE2 Centre. After being grilled by an expert panel of judges, the top awards were given to two 17-year-olds. Peter Hatfield from Kent was pronounced Young Scientist of the Year, while Chris Jefferies from Worcestershire was awarded the title of Young Technologist. Peter astonished judges with his blueprint for a cosmic ray detector, a tiny gadget that will be sent into orbit in 2010. Chris claimed his victory with a special device that can detect damage to the equipment used to test gearboxes. Now the lads will be 'ambassadors for science' – helping other young people to develop new innovations that could change the future for everyone. Over 6,500 people visited the Fair - now organisers hope that visitors' minds are buzzing with ideas for Big Bang 2010, due to be held in Manchester.

TRIUMPHS OF TECHNOLOGY?

A host of new technological advances catch our attention every year. Some might not make it into our homes, but the concepts behind them often inspire new inventions that can change our lives for the better.

The Heart Robot

Designer David McGoran's new puppet robot showed that droids are getting more humanised. The Heart Robot has a breathing chest and heart that slows down and relaxes when it is cuddled. It can also respond to movement, noise and touch.

Sixth Sense

In April 2009 tech experts presented a device that allows people to go online just by using their hands. The Sixth Sense gadget is worn around your neck – when you're ready to surf you just make a rectangle on any flat surface. The device is a projector connected to a hi-tech mobile phone, allowing users to search the net wherever and whenever they want.

Projector phone

Similar projector technology has been used to get around the problem of mobile phones having small screens. New projector phones are able to beam pictures, video and games onto the wall, so you can share them with a crowd of friends. The only hitch? The projector only works in a darkened room.

RuBot II

The famous Rubik's Cube is no challenge for Pete Redmond's latest invention. 'The Cubinator' has been fitted with cameras in its eyes, allowing it to solve the colour puzzle in less than 50 seconds.

Speed Searcher

Four boys from Buckinghamshire won the Innovation Nation award with a new gadget that can track down lost trainers. The Speed Searcher uses software implanted in your shoes that acts as an easy locator device whenever you need to find them in a hurry!

GAMING GADGETS

Addicted to your Wii, DS or PlayStation? The future looked exciting for all gaming nuts at July 2008's E3 conference. All the big name console companies came to the US seminar, ready to present their hottest new ideas.

New Wii controller

Nintendo showed off its new MotionPlus gadget. The handheld controller is ultra-sensitive – adding more realistic movement to its games.

Films on the PS3

Sony unveiled a film download service for North American Playstation 3 users, plus a much larger capacity.

In the longer term there are hints that handheld gaming might be about to transform altogether. In September 2008, Ricky Boleto met an American company that will allow users to play just by using the power of their minds! The NeuroSky headset is fitted with special sensors that detect activity in your brain. Just by concentrating, players can move around a virtual world and make their on-screen character follow commands.

Us and the universe

THE DAY THAT THE WORLD WAS GOING TO END

Journalists and newsreaders held their breath on 10th September 2008. It was the start of an important experiment using a mammoth piece of equipment called the Large Hadron Collider. By re-creating conditions at the start of the universe, they hoped that their work might uncover how the world began. People were worried about the scale of the experiment however. Some even claimed that the Earth might get sucked into a giant black hole at the moment that the Collider was turned on! Luckily their fears didn't come true.

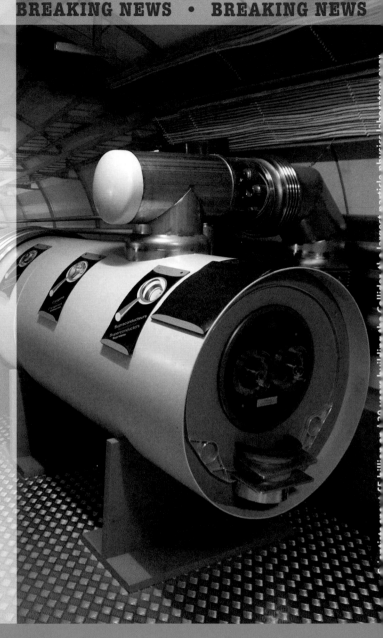

KNOW YOUR STUFF

How the Hadron works

Many scientists believe that the universe was formed when tiny particles smashed into each other and joined to make planets. Sometimes this is known as the Big Bang theory. The Large Hadron Collider has been built to test the idea out.

Scientists built a 27 kilometre tunnel deep underground near the Swiss city of Geneva. Over 1,000 magnets were fitted inside. Next they set up a beam of tiny particles that could travel up and down the tunnel at extreme speed. When the particles whiz around fast enough, scientists will observe what happens when they bang into each other.

The Hadron Collider got off to a great start. Unfortunately, 10 days later, the equipment broke down. It seems that some of the magnets inside stopped working properly, causing damage to the underground pipe. Experts thought it could be fixed quickly, but in December 2008 they announced that it would need £14 million worth of repairs. The experiment is scheduled to restart in Summer 2009.

CRAZY CROP CIRCLES

The UK was baffled in June 2008 when the most complex crop circle ever was discovered in Wiltshire. Crop circles are strange patterns that appear overnight in fields. The massive design mind-boggled experts when it revealed a detailed number code - the first ten digits of a famous formula called pi. No one can explain how it got there.

STRANGE SIGHTINGS

UFO sightings are reported every year and 2008 was no exception. When some new Ministry of Defence files were released in October however, they made interesting reading. The files published a series of UFO sightings that took place between 1986 and 1992.

One report said that the pilot of a plane in 1991 had to shout out to his co-pilot after spotting a brown, missile-shaped object out of his window. Even though the Ministry Defence was never able to explain the sighting, the investigation was soon closed.

In January 2009 another mystery hit the headlines. A wind turbine in Lincolnshire was found with one blade bent and another one broken off. Local residents had been calling the police to report bright lights in the sky nearby. The owners of the turbine were stumped. Could it have been little green men? Most scientists think that it was probably caused by frozen rainwater getting into cracks in the blades, but UFOs haven't been ruled out.

In the news

Is there anybody out there?

In March 2009 a giant telescope was blasted into space. Its mission? To search the galaxy to find planets that might be capable of supporting life.

The Kepler telescope (picture above) will spend three and a half years touring space. It's expected to search more than 100,000 stars to find out if they are orbited by Earth-like planets. It's a long shot because conditions have to be just right for any kind of life to survive. In order to create the right conditions, planets need to be the perfect distance from their nearest star so that it isn't too hot or too cold.

The Kepler team aren't expecting to find aliens. Instead they hope to chance upon planets that show signs that they could support living things such as tiny bacteria.

You could also stick or clip, newspaper cuttings or pictures that you'd like to keep.

FAMOUS FOR BEING FAMOUS

Is it possible that we became even more fame obsessed in 2008? Society has always honoured certain people for their particular skill or talent, but in recent times our fascination with the rich and famous has grown so much we now want to know every tiny detail of their private lives. This has led to the rise of a new breed of celebrities: people who are famous simply for being famous. These people are rarely off the front pages, but we often can't remember what they do or why they deserve to be there.

Peaches and Pixie Geldof, who have celebrity parents, are now also famous themselves.

Jade Goody

Once admitting "I know I'm famous for nothing", Jade Goody was perhaps the best-known example of someone famous for being famous. Love her or hate her, we became mesmerized by her story and couldn't help but be moved by her tragic death from cancer on Mother's Day 2009. She was just 27 and leaves behind two sons aged 4 and 5. Jade shot to stardom in 2002 after coming fourth on Channel 4 Reality TV show *Big Brother*. She was originally mocked for saying things like 'East Angular' instead of East Anglia, but people warmed to her down-to-earth nature and she became a household name.

Although she was criticised for living her life and particularly her final months in the media spotlight, she was determined to earn enough money to secure a stable future for her children, and many people admired the brave way she dealt with her fate. Her legacy will be raising awareness of cervical cancer.

WEB CHECK Click on the Showbiz icon on the

Alexandra Burke, the winner of 2008's The *X Factor* poses with Newsround's Ricky Boleto.

Talent shows rule UK

It seems we can't get enough of programmes which prove how much (or little) talent we have. This year, shows such as *Britain's Got Talent*, *The X-Factor*, *Dancing on Ice* and *Strictly Come Dancing*, dominated our screens and brought us the good, the bad and the downright odd.

On the plus side we were introduced to exciting new talent in our midst, such as street dancer George Sampson and singer Alexandra Burke. We also learnt that some celebrities had other strings to their bows. But while displays of true talent are impressive, at the other end of the scale, the more bizarre antics of some entrants divide opinion. Overweight *The X-Factor* auditionee Emma Chawner came back in 2008 after just six singing lessons only to be ridiculed by the Judges once more. This led people to question the value and ethics of such shows. For some, like *The X-Factor* winner Leona Lewis (now commanding a £1m fee for a 30-minute performance), they provide the showbiz fairytale, but for many (including 2007 winner Leon Jackson, who this year was dropped by his record label Sony BMG) they can be a route to shattered dreams.

• PRESS PACK REPORT •

'I love to sing and last year I decided to audition for *Britain's Got Talent*. My mum didn't know anything about it until the application form arrived, but she said she'd support me if I wanted to try. We queued up for ages on the day and then I got called into a small room, but instead of the judges it was just two people from the production team watching me. I only sang for about 30 seconds, then they said thank you, we'll get back to you in a week if you're through, and then you'll perform for the judges. I waited and waited for the call but no-one rang. I felt a bit down at first but now I feel happy I didn't go on stage in case everyone booed me. Sometimes, watching the show I feel upset for people who get laughed at – they've got guts to go up there.'

Caitlin Dempster, 11, Glasgow.

HIGHS AND LOWS

It's always nice to see pampered celebrities working to improve the lives of others. Here are some of the ways our more caring stars gave back to the public in 2008 and 2009.

Inspiring stars

Chef Jamie Oliver continued his crusade for healthy eating in 2008 with new series *Jamie's Ministry of Food*. The aim being to teach us how to cook, pass on recipes and therefore eat more healthily. In the US, where he is also a big name, he became a judge on Oprah Winfrey's show *The Big Give* where 10 contestants are given the money and resources to find ways to help other people.

In March 2009 a team of nine stars (pictured in the photograph above) including Cheryl Cole, Fearne Cotton and Gary Barlow trekked their way up to the summit of Mount Kilimanjaro in aid of Comic Relief. It was tough – they suffered symptoms of altitude sickness – but they raised over £1.5 million.

Presenter and actress Amanda Holden and her rescue dog Fudge spearheaded the Pedigree dog Adoption Drive and walked the first leg of a mammoth relay from Lands End to John o'Groats in March 2009. The sponsored dog walk aimed to raise £600,000 for rescue charities across the UK. Around 100,000 dogs are abandoned or stray in the UK each year, but figures are climbing due to the recession.

Coldplay frontman Chris Martin is well known for his support for Fairtrade, but in February 2009 he helped organise a concert to take place directly after the Brit Awards. The amazing line-up included The Killers, Coldplay, Bono and Gary Barlow, with interval entertainment by Al Murray. All proceeds from the concert and the album *Heroes* went to War Child – a charity which helps children affected by conflict in places like Afghanistan, Iraq and The Republic of Congo.

Presenter scandals

Several of our more famous presenters hit the headlines this year for all the wrong reasons, leading to accusations that they are overpaid and out of control:

Jonathan Ross and Russell Brand were both suspended by the BBC for leaving a tasteless message on a famous actor's phone during their radio show.

Radio Presenter Chris Moyles was reprimanded by broadcast watchdog Ofcom over 'stereotypical and negative' jokes about singer Will Young.

Hosts Ant and Dec (pictured below with Robbie Williams) were twice caught up in controversy, albeit not of their making. In 2008 they gave back their 2005 'People's Choice' British Comedy Award, after it emerged organisers had fixed the phone-in in favour of them, rather than Catherine Tate. This was allegedly done in order to lure Robbie Williams as a presenter. Early in 2009 accusations about rigged voting on their shows *Saturday Night Takeaway and Game Show* ended in Ofcom ruling that ITV plc pay a record £5,675,000 fine for the abuse of premium-rate services.

The pitfalls of fame

It's not always rosy on planet celeb – some stars struggle with the pressures of constant scrutiny. In 2008 we witnessed pop sensation Britney Spears (pictured above) suffer a very public melt-down which began when she shaved her head. The year ended with her being sectioned and losing custody of her two children to ex-husband, rapper Kevin Federline. Other stars struggling with fame include Amy Winehouse, whose battle with drugs has been much publicised; Kerry Katona, who slurred her way through a TV series and an interview on daytime TV; and Lily Allen, who got drunk and disorderly at two award ceremonies. Other stars under fire this year include those who were criticised in the press over their yo-yoing weight such as ex-Eastender Natalie Cassidy and singer Jessica Simpson.

NEW CELEBRITY KIDS ON THE BLOCK

The celebrity stork has been working overtime in 2008 and 2009 with A-listers including J-Lo, Christina Aguilera and former Spice Girl Mel C all becoming first-time mums. As usual, the stars have gone for some weird and wonderful names. How will their kids get on in the playground?

Nicole Richie and Joel Madden had daughter *Harlow Winter Kate* (top right) on 11 January 2008.

Halle Berry and boyfriend Gabriel Aubr gave birth to daughter *Nahla Ariela* on 16 March 2008.

Actress Cate Blanchett and husband Andrew Upton had third son *Ignatius* on 13 April 2008.

Radio 1 DJ Edith Bowman and boyfriend Tom Smith had son *Rudy Brae* on 10 June 2008.

Nicole Kidman and husband Keith Urban had a girl called *Sunday Rose* (middle right) on 7 July 2008.

Singer Gwen Stefani and husband Gavin Rossdale welcomed son *Zuma Nesta Rock* (bottom right) on 21 August 2008.

Newsreader Natasha Kaplinsky and husband Justin Bower had son *Arlo* on 25 September 2008.

Actress Billie Piper and husband Laurence Fox gave birth to a boy, *Winston James*, on 21 October 2008.

Singer Ashlee Simpson, sister of Jessica, and husband Pete Wentz had son *Bronx Mowgli* on 20 November 2008.

Actors Jennifer Garner and Ben Affleck had their second daughter *Seraphina* on 6 January 2009.

Explorer Bear Grylls and wife Shara had their third child, *Huckleberry Edward Jocelyn*, on 15 January 2009.

Singer Sophie Ellis-Bexter and husband Richard had their second child, a son, *Kit Valentine*, on 7 February 2009.

Top showbiz gossip stories!

1 Madonna's divorce

In August 2008, the Queen of Pop and her film director husband, Guy Ritchie, ended months of speculation about their eight-year marriage by announcing a divorce. They avoided an undignified court battle over Madonna's millions, and the Material Girl's love affair with all things British seems well and truly over. She moved back to New York immediately and began dating a Brazilian model.

2 Britney's roller coaster year

Things reached a real low when the pop star was sectioned, having dated a member of the paparazzi. Later Britney managed to stage an amazing comeback with a number one album, *Circus,* and a world tour.

3 Heath Ledger dies

In January 2008, Hollywood was rocked by the death of the actor who was found dead in his hotel room aged just 28. Audiences grieved the loss of his talent when his last film *The Dark Knight* was released, revealing an Oscar-winning performance by Heath as The Joker.

4 The Miley Cyrus scandal

Miley Cyrus, star of Disney's *Hannah Montana* had a rough ride in the press in June 2008 when photographs from a shoot by legendary photographer Annie Liebowitz appeared on the cover of *Vanity Fair* magazine. The black and white shots of the star wrapped in just a sheet proved too risqué. Many people deemed them inappropriate and she was forced to issue an apology to her fans.

5 Brangelina Twins

July 2008 saw the arrival of the most eagerly anticipated babies on the planet. Angelina Jolie gave birth to twins Vivienne and Knox by partner Brad Pitt in Nice, France. They then sold the first photos of the babies for a reported $14 million, donating the lot to charity.

6 John Sergeant on Strictly

John Sergeant became a national treasure with his hopeless performances on Strictly Come Dancing. The judges begged viewers to vote him off, but the public kept him in. In the end he quit, admitting "The trouble is that there is now a real danger I might win the competition. Even for me that would be taking a joke too far." Around 170,000 posts from fans protesting about his departure clogged up the Strictly messageboard, which had to be temporarily shut down.

7 Twilight is released

When release of *Harry Potter and the Half Blood Prince* was delayed until summer 2009, the makers of *Twilight* jumped in. The adaptation of Stephanie Meyer's vampire tale took more than $100 million in its first week and made an instant heart-throb of British actor Robert Pattinson, who played Cedric Diggory in Harry Potter.

8 Madge adoption battle

The world raised its eyebrows when Madonna decided in early 2009 to adopt another child. The singer, who has two biological children, Lourdes and Rocco, also has an adopted son from Malawi called David. Her plans to adopt a daughter, Mercy, from Malawi caused many arguments. Some say that as a rich star she can provide a great home for a child while organisations such as Save The Children believe that it's always better for orphans to be cared for in their own country.

The death of Australian actor Heath Ledger shocked many people.

In production

Film fans are set for a great 2009 and beyond. Stuart Brown of the British Film Institute suggests you look out for the following releases…

Where The Wild Things Are
Spike Jonze's adaptation of the classic book by Maurice Sendak.

Up
The new Pixar Film about an old man who ties hundreds of balloons to his house to travel to South America.

The Princess and the Frog
The first 2D animation from Disney in five years and the first to feature a mixed-race love story.

Fantastic Mr Fox
Animation of the Roald Dahl tale, featuring the voices of George Clooney and Cate Blanchett as Mr and Mrs Fox.

Alvin and the Chipmunks: The Squeakuel
Set for release at Christmas, it's rumoured to feature the voices of Miley Cyrus and Drew Barrymore as brand new characters.

A Christmas Carol
Robert Zemeckis, the mastermind from The Polar Express teams up with Jim Carrey.

And 2010 treats include **How to Train your Dragon**, an animation based on the Cressida Cowell book; **Harry Potter and the Deathly Hallows: Part I**; **Toy Story 3** and **Alice in Wonderland**, the latest Tim Burton offering with Johnny Depp as The Mad Hatter and Ann Hathaway as the White Queen.

A TRIUMPHANT YEAR FOR UK FILM

The cast of *Slumdog Millionaire* pose for the cameras.

What an incredible year it's been for British film. At the 2009 Golden Globes, Kate Winslet became the first-ever actress to take home the award for Best Actress and Best Supporting Actress on the same night. British film *Slumdog Millionnaire* also won four Globes. A month later we had our biggest Oscar haul ever. *Slumdog* lifted eight Oscars while Winslet, having been the actress most nominated without winning, at last received the gold statuette for Best Actress (*The Reader*).

RISING UK TALENT

Teens on Screen

With the Harry Potter stars entering their 20s and the series coming to an end, there's no reason to stop visiting your cinema. Here we introduce the next big teen stars to gild the silver screen…

Robbie Kay
The 13-year-old, from Tyneside, appeared in *Hannibal Rising* and TV drama *My Boy Jack* with Daniel Radcliffe. He recently made the shortlist in Hollywood's Young Artist Awards, nominated for Best Performance in an International Feature Film for *Fugitive Pieces* and for Best Performance in a TV Movie for his role in *Pinocchio* opposite Bob Hoskins.

Dakota Blue Richards
At just 13, this Brighton teenager was plucked from obscurity to star in *The Secret of Moonacre*. In 2006 she beat thousands of hopefuls to the part of Lyra Belacqua in *The Golden Compass*, shooting her into the big league. Now 15, her next drama is *Five Miles Out*.

Eliza Bennett
The pretty 17-year-old, from Reading cracked the West End with a role in 'Chitty Chitty Bang Bang'. She made the move into film with a small part in *The Prince and Me* and since then has worked with the likes of Colin Firth and Emma Thompson in *Nanny McPhee,* and Helen Mirren and Brendan Fraser in *Inkheart*. See her next in *From Time to Time* opposite Maggie Smith and Timothy Spall.

Thomas Turgoose
This talented actor, 17, won the British Independent Film Awards 2006 honour for Most Promising Newcomer for his performance in *This is England*. This year he went on to win The London Critic's Circle Young British Performance of the Year for *Somers Town/Eden Lake*. See him next in *The Scouting Book for Boys*.

Also on the up … Freddie Highmore, 17, star of *Spiderwick Chronicles*; Jemma McKenzie Brown, 19, star of *HSM 3*; Thomas Sangster,18, star of *Love Actually* and *Nanny McPhee*.

Thomas Turgoose

Dakota Blue Richards

Eliza Bennett

ENDINGS AND NEW BEGINNINGS ON CBBC

It's been a year of flux and change on the small screen. We've said goodbye to some classic shows, greeted new faces and welcomed back old friends.

Some of the 1980s cast of Grange Hill which was cancelled in 2008.

Beaker's back

In March 2008 we learnt that *Tracy Beaker*, the youngster-in-care character created by Jacqueline Wilson, would be back on our screens in 2010 as an adult carer herself. Dani Harmer, now 20, who as a youngster played Beaker for five years, will reprise the role.

Goodbye Grange Hill

In February 2008 the school drama was axed after 30 years on air. The series began on 8 February 1978 and featured tough storylines about social issues including drugs and teenage pregnancy. In the 1980s, at the height of its popularity, stars of the show fronted an anti-drugs campaign, even releasing a single and meeting President Reagan's wife Nancy at the White House. However, times have changed, and CBBC controller Anne Gilchrist said, "The lives of children have changed a great deal since *Grange Hill* began and we owe it to them to reflect this. We mustn't confuse our own nostalgia for something that we loved for something that children want nowadays."

Dr Who?

In October 2008, David Tennant stunned Who fans by announcing his departure from the series while accepting the Outstanding Drama Performance prize at the National Television Awards. Then in the New Year there was more surprise when his successor was revealed as the virtually unknown 26-year-old Matt Smith. Headlines screamed 'Dr Who?' and 'Toddler in the Tardis!'. Now the young actor has to prove that he can fill Tennant's shoes.

In the news

HAPPY BIRTHDAY HOMER

TV's most dysfunctional animated family, *The Simpsons*, celebrated their 20th birthday in 2008.

The Simpsons became a must-see show in 1990 and has remained one of the most groundbreaking and innovative series to this day. It is also the longest-running primetime sitcom in television history. The occasion was marked with the release in April 2009 of a set of stamps immortalising characters Homer, Marge, Bart, Lisa and Maggie. It truly is an honour as the US Postal Service receives about 50,000 stamp suggestions per year.

BREAKTHROUGH TALENT

In November 2008 The Breakthrough Talent Award at the Children's British Academy of Film and Television Arts awards (BAFTAs) went to Clifton teenager Eliot-Otis Brown Walters. At 15, he already has an impressive CV that includes appearances on *The Bill*, *Doctors* and, more recently, CBBC drama *Summerhill*.

MUSIC NEWS

According to official sales figures, Duffy and Alexandra Burke were the UK's top-selling musicians of the year.

In the final two weeks of 2008, *The X Factor* winner Burke sold 888,000 copies of her version of 'Hallelujah' to take the year's biggest-selling single. Duffy's debut album *Rockferry* held off a late challenge from Take That's *Circus* to make it to top of the year-end chart, with 1.685 million copies sold.

Kings of Leon, Leona Lewis and Coldplay all sold over a million albums in 2008. Official Charts Company (OCC) data shows *The X Factor* finalists' version of 'Hero' was the year's second biggest-selling single, shifting 751,000 copies. Duffy's 'Mercy' sold 536,000 copies, the only other single to sell over half a million.

The *Mamma Mia* soundtrack sold 1.007 million copies the year's top compilation.

o read reviews on the latests chart singles and albums and TV shows.

IS THERE A NEW JK ROWLING?

For the first time this decade, the book charts were not based around huge sales of the latest Harry Potter. The series has ended, but fans still had their fix with new JK Rowling book *The Tales of Beedle the Bard*. The real story of 2008 came courtesy of Stephenie Meyer, an American author whose books *Eclipse*, *Breaking Dawn* and the film adaptation of *Twilight* made her a worldwide star. Her books now represent 1.8% of the children's book market, while Rowling's represent 1.9%. Could she possibly top the children's chart next year?

JK Rowling's The Tales of Beedle the Bard sold over 850,000 copies in 2008.

BE INSPIRED

Libby Rees, 13, explains how she got published:
'My first book *Help, Hope and Happiness* came about because my parents got divorced when I was six and I figured out my own ways to cope. When I was nine I wrote down my tips and, with the help of Mum, sent my manuscript off to about 30 publishers. I never expected to hear anything, but the next day I got a call from the publishing house Script, asking if I'd like to sign a contract. In 2008, my second book *At Sixes and Sevens* was published. It's about going from primary to secondary school. I write about issues I know about and experiences I've been through. I would advise anyone wanting to write to do the same and also to just get going rather than putting pressure on yourself by thinking about the whole book, or telling yourself you must finish it by a certain time.

The best thing about being a published author has been the doors it's opened for me. A portion of the money from sales goes to Save the Children and I'm now one of their Youth Ambassadors. I sit on panels and have even given presentations at 10 Downing Street and Buckingham Palace. It's a great opportunity to make a difference.'

TOP 10 OF EVERYTHING 2008

Top 10 Bestselling Albums
1. *Rockferry* – **Duffy**
2. *The Circus* – **Take That**
3. *Only By The Night* – **Kings of Leon**
4. *Spirit* – **Leona Lewis**
5. *Viva La Vida...* – **Coldplay**
6. *Good Girl Gone Bad* – **Rihanna**
7. *Day and Age* – **Killers**
8. *Out of Control* – **Girls Aloud**
9. *Funhouse* – **Pink**
10. *Scouting for Girls* – **Scouting for Girls**

Top 10 Bestselling Singles
1. 'Hallelujah' – **Alexandra Burke**
2. 'Hero' – *The X Factor* **finalists**
3. 'Mercy' – **Duffy**
4. 'I Kissed A Girl' – **Katy Perry**
5. 'Rockstar' – **Nickelback**
6. 'American Boy' – **Estelle/ Kanye West**
7. 'Sex on Fire' – **Kings of Leon**
8. 'Now You're Gone' – **Basshunter**
9. '4 Minutes' – **Madonna/ Justin Timberlake**
10. 'Black and Gold' – **Sam Sparro**

Top 10 Family Films of 2008
(based on worldwide box office figures)
1. *Indiana Jones and the Kingdom of the Crystal Skull*
2. *Kung Fu Panda*
3. *Madagascar 2*
4. *Wall-E*
5. *Chronicles of Narnia: Prince Caspian*
6. *Twilight*
7. *Horton Hears a Who*
8. *Bolt*
9. *Hulk*
10. *High School Musical 3: The Movie*

Top 10 Bestselling Games
(all formats)
1. *FIFA 09 EA*
2. *Mario Kart Wii*
3. *GTA IV*
4. *Mario and Sonic at the Olympic Games*
5. *Wii Fit*
6. *Call of Duty: World at War*
7. *Wii Play*
8. *Dr Kawashima's Brain Training*
9. *Lego Indiana Jones*
10. *Carnival Funfair*

Top 10 Children's Fiction 2008
1. *Tales of Beedle the Bard* – **JK Rowling**
2. *Twilight* – **Stephenie Meyer**
3. *The Boy in the Striped Pyjamas* – **John Boyne**
4. *New Moon* – **Stephenie Meyer**
5. *Brisingr* – **Christopher Paolini**
6. *Eclipse* – **Stephenie Meyer**
7. *Nation* – **Terry Pratchett**
8. *Breaking Dawn* – **Stephenie Meyer**
9. *Horrid Henry Robs the Bank* – **Francesca Simon**
10. *Cookie* – **Jacqueline Wilson**

In early 2009 you were mostly reading Captain Underpants and the Attack of the Talking Toilets, Tracy Beaker's Thumping Heart, Horrible Histories, MrGum and Beast Quest.

In the UK, the films you spent most of your pocket money seeing were:
Indiana Jones - £40,088,636
Wall-E - £22,772,269
HSM 3 - £22,739,722
Kung Fu Panda - £20,044,229
Madagascar 2 - £17,958,254

Top 10 Children's Annuals
1. Disney High School Musical
2. Doctor Who
3. The Beano
4. Hannah Montana
5. Top Gear
6. Ben 10
7. In the Night Garden
8. Horrid Henry
9. WWE
10. Disney Princess

Books to look out for....

Ghost Hunter by Michelle Paver. The final title in the Chronicles of Ancient Darkness sequence.

Horrid Henry Wakes the Dead by Francesca Simon. Brand new stories from everyone's favourite horrid little boy!

Scat by Carl Hiaasen. Eco-thriller set in Florida's Everglades.

The Egyptian Chronicles: The Spitting Cobra and The Horned Viper by Gill Harvey. First and second installments of a new series set in Ancient Egypt.

Madame Pamplemousse and the Time-Travelling Café by Rupert Kingfisher. Parisien café owner, Monsieur Moutarde has a large, silver, expresso coffee machine on his bar, which brews a liquid to help drinkers travel through time.

Al Capone Shines My Shoes by Gennifer Choldenko. The second title to feature Moose Flanagan and his friends on Alcatraz.

Shine On, Daizy Star by Cathy Cassidy. Daizy's dad is hatching a mad-cap plan that is going to throw her life into chaos!

Your entertainment

YOUR ENTERTAINMENT Use this page to write your own entertainment stories and information.

Ricky Boleto

1 Describe your path into presenting Newsround?
Since I was about 7 I knew that I wanted to work in news. I've worked pretty hard to crack the industry and make my way into reporting. To get there I spent three years at university studying journalism. After that I completed work experience at a number of places including Sky News. Luckily, that led to a job at Five News where I started as a researcher behind the scenes. Eventually, I made it onto the screen as Five's youngest ever reporter and presenter. Two years later I ended up at my dream job, here at Newsround.

2 Which of the past year's news stories particularly struck a chord with you?
Personal stories are always the most powerful and the ones that stick in my mind. The bush fires in Australia was a good example of that. So many people lost their lives trying to escape the flames, so Newsround sent me to cover the story. We spent a week hearing from children who had lost everything they own including their schools.

3 Was there anything you found difficult to cover and how do you cope with negative or distressing stories?
After the bush fires many people were living in make-shift tents until they could rebuild their lives. It was very hard to speak to some of the children who had just lost their personal belongings and pets. Some of the kids had even lost their best friends in the fires. It can be very difficult, but you have to remain professional even when the story is really emotional.

4 What do you do in a typical day?
There's hardly ever a typical day in the Newsround office! Each day can throw up a lot of surprises. I could be on a train one day or on a plane the next. Usually the team gets together in the morning to talk about what stories we are going to cover on TV and online. The producer assigns me with a story and a camera person. After that, it's my job to run around and speak to all the people we need before the story gets put together by an editor then broadcast on Newsround and published online.

Ricky was in Australia to report on the terrible bush fires.

WEB CHECK Find out more about the team at http://news.bbc.co.uk/cbbcnews/hi/the_team

Ricky, out and about, reporting for Newsround.

5 **What's the most exciting thing about your job?**
Being able to meet interesting and important people. I really enjoy being on the red carpet at music awards and speaking to some of the celebrities. Plus I get to visit places I've never been before and chat to some really cool children. Sometimes you get spotted when you are out and about, and that can be really fun too.

6 **Are there any downsides to being a news reporter/presenter?**
Lots of people think being on TV is all fun and games, but it's really demanding and tiring. Often, you get very tight deadlines and not enough time to do everything, but I wouldn't change it for the world.

7 **Have you had any on-screen disasters so far?**
Yes! I tried to read some breaking news out during one of the bulletins. It didn't come out properly and I ended up looking really silly. Another time I got a bit star struck speaking to top singer Duffy at the Brits. I asked her a question which didn't make sense. She just looked at me and laughed and I went bright red!

8 **What is it like working in a newsroom when a story breaks?**
Working in a newsroom is really exciting. We have lots of TV's on in the office, broadcasting different news channels. The minute a news story breaks you can feel the buzz and energy inside the office. Every day you feel part of the news and the real challenge is to get that story all wrapped up and onto your screens!

The 2008 Olympics

THE GREATEST SHOW ON EARTH

Beijing was rarely out of the news in 2008. In the run-up to the Games, the Olympic Torch travelled 140,000 kilometres to China's Bird Nest Stadium in the capital. Along the way, parades in France, America and the UK were disrupted by protesters unhappy with the Chinese government's treatmen of Tibet. Despite this, the Beijing organisers gave the world a spectacular opening ceremony and went on to showcase some of the most thrilling sports performances for years.

COOL FACTS

When the action started on August 2008, the Beijing Olympic and Paralympic Games had the world gripped. Newsround's Sonali Shah was one of thousands of reporters who witnessed the event.

Here are some impressive facts and stats:

- A staggering 3.5 billion people watched the Games on TV.
- Over 10,500 athletes competed. A record 87 countries won at least one gold medal.
- The Olympics featured 28 separate sports, with 20 in the Paralympics.
- More than 21,000 journalists were posted in China to cover the competition.

KNOW YOUR STUFF

The dark side of the Games

China worked hard to have the perfect Games, but organisers were criticised.

Out of air
Athletes were worried about the air quality in Beijing. The city is smoggy, making it hard for sports people to perform. When Ethiopian marathon runner Haile Gebrselassie pulled out, the Chinese authorities began a clean-up campaign to sort it out.

Child labour
The Chinese government was embarrassed when a story emerged that the goods being manufactured to promote the Games were made in factories using child workers. China furiously denied these claims.

Simply too strict
Nearly a million Games representatives went round the city, telling its citizens that they shouldn't hug in public, go out in pyjamas or shake hands for longer than three seconds!

Beautiful people only
At the opening ceremony a sweet-looking 9-year-old girl – Lin Miaoke sang. Later it turned out that Lin was miming to the voice of Yang Peiyi. They had decided that Yang wasn't pretty enough, so they drafted in Lin instead!

Team GB

The months before the Games were a nervous time for British athletes waiting to find out if they'd made the Olympic squad. Sadly, disappointment waited for some. Zara Phillips, the world eventing champion, pulled out because her horse Toytown got injured. Heptathlete Jessica Ennis also withdrew after hurting her ankle. Paula Radcliffe was injured and did make it to Beijing, but had to run through the pain to take 23rd place in the Olympic Marathon.

AWE-INSPIRING ATHLETES

Every day in Beijing brought excitement. There were amazing Olympic firsts and record-breaking performances on the track, in the gym, velodrome and the pool. It was Great Britain's most successful games, with the teams coming fourth in the Olympics and second in the Paralympics. The most outstanding individual performance was by American, Michael Phelps (pictured above). When the swimmer got a 14th gold medal he became the Greatest Olympian of all time. The trailblazer earned eight golds during Beijing.

Sweet victory

In 2008, Team GB exceeded expectations. Nicole Cooke won the team's first gold medal in Beijing, in the women's road bike race. Although most medals were won in cycling, swimming and rowing, the team achieved great things in many new arenas.

Gymnastics
When he claimed a bronze for the pommel horse, Louis Smith became the first British male to win a medal in an individual event in the gymnastics for 80 years!

Women's 400 metres
Christine Ohuruogu claimed Britain's 16th Olympic gold medal. She also hit the history books by becoming the first British woman to win the Olympic 400 metre race.

Men's cycling
Scotland's Chris Hoy became a cycling legend. The athlete became the first Briton to win three gold medals in a Games for 100 years!

On the edge of our seats

Perhaps Beijing was so watchable because the events were often tense and full of drama. Even minor sports grabbed the headlines, such as GB's Sarah Stevenson's performance in the martial arts event, tae kwon do. In the quarter finals, the athlete was told that she had lost her fight because the judges missed one of her kicks. Sarah and her coach appealed and for the first time ever, the result was overturned. Although Sarah lost in the semis, she beat Noha Abd Rabo to win Britain's first ever bronze in the sport.

A celebration of the Olympic spirit

No matter what was happening outside of Beijing, the athletes put aside differences to support each other. The Olympic Village were delighted when Irving Saladino from Panama won first place in the long jump. It was the nation's first ever gold and his homeland was so impressed it decided to name a sports complex after him!

Sonali Shah reported from right inside Beijing's Bird Nest Stadium.

London's Mayor Boris Johnson steps up to the podium at the 2008 Summer Olympics. He said that he was 'lost in admiration and awe for the achievements of the British team.'

GLORY FOR GB

The 2008 Summer Olympics finished in the same dazzling fashion as they had begun. After the Games had ended, the Team GB heroes were given a victory parade through the streets of London. It was Britain's most medal-laden Olympics for 100 years, with 19 gold, 13 silver and 15 bronze. The athletes surpassed the medal targets they had been set for the London Olympics in 2012! The Paralympics team notched up even more accolades, amassing an impressive haul of 102 medals.

Three cheers for Ellie

One of Team GB's most popular heroes of the Paralympics was young swimmer Eleanor Simmonds.

She won double gold in the 100 metre and 400 metre freestyle events, even though she was just 13! Eleanor is Britain's youngest ever individual gold medallist. She even surprised herself saying, 'I didn't believe I would be able to do that.'

In the Autumn, Eleanor was named the BBC Young Sports Personality of the Year and put on the Queen's Honour's List. Her MBE from Her Majesty marks another first, making her the youngest person to ever be placed on the list.

The best games ever?

At the end of the Games, over 90,000 people attended the glittering closing parade inside the Birds Nest Stadium. A host of world leaders including Prime Minister Gordon Brown flew in to watch the ceremony. Towards the end a red doubledecker bus was driven into the arena to symbolise the move to the 2012 Olympics in London. There were also appearances from Leona Lewis and David Beckham.

The stuff of dreams

All the Olympic athletes had spent years training so that they could shine during their big moment at Beijing. Here are some of the British sportsmen and women that proved they had the golden touch:

Rebecca Adlington
The ace swimmer won the nation's heart when she claimed gold in both the 800 metre and 400 metre freestyle events.

Ben Ainslie
The determined athlete helped himself to his third gold medal in Beijing, making him one of Britain's most successful Olympic sailors ever.

Rebecca Romero
Two years before the Games Rebecca had been focusing on a rowing career. Luckily she decided to switch to cycling in time to earn gold in Beijing.

Bradley Wiggins
Bradley's two cycling golds in China took his total medal tally over the last three Olympics to an enviable six.

Chris Hoy
After his three Beijing gold medals, cyclist Hoy went on to become the much-deserved 2008 BBC Sports Personality of the Year.

London 2012 Olympics

THE RACE TO 2012

In July 2005 London beat Paris to win the bid to host the next Olympic Games. Now the spotlight has shifted to East London where the Games will be held. The area is being regenerated, equipped with an Olympic Village for the athletes to stay in, plus top sports facilities. Sebastian Coe, the chairman of the London 2012 Organising Committee, is in charge of making sure that everything is ready for the opening ceremony on 27th July 2012.

A blow for minor sports

In March 2009, it was announced that eight sports would lose £50 million of funding, in an effort to channel money into Team GB's most successful events. The unlucky sports were:

Volleyball • Shooting • Table tennis
Handball • Fencing • Water polo
Wrestling • Weightlifting

Britain didn't win any medals at these events at Beijing, prompting the decision to spend the money elsewhere.

KNOW YOUR STUFF

Where will it happen?

The showpiece of the Games will be the Olympic Stadium in Stratford. The arena will be surrounded by water on three sides, and will have enough seats for 80,000 people. After the Games are over it is expected to be partly dismantled and turned into a 25,000 seater venue. With sports ranging from gymnastics to basketball, a host of other venues will also be used. Here are some of the most exciting:

The Aquatics Centre
This water venue will be the gateway to the Olympic Park. Inside there will be a 50 metre pool, a 25 metre diving pool and a 50 metre training pool.

The Velopark
This site will be made up of a modern velodrome and a BMX circuit. It is going to be built on the site of a 100-year-old rubbish tip!

Greenwich Park
All of the horse-riding events will take place in London's oldest Royal Park, in front of the Royal Observatory.

Lord's Cricket Ground
The outfield and nursery ground of this historic pitch is going to host a temporary archery range.

The O2 Arena
Gymnastics, basketball and wheelchair basketball will take place in the old Millennium Dome.

Wembley Stadium
What better venue for Olympic football than Britain's iconic new stadium with its dazzling white arch? There will also be football at other UK grounds such as Old Trafford in Manchester and Hampden Park in Glasgow.

Wimbledon
The world-famous courts at Wimbledon once hosted Olympic tennis in 1908, but are being renovated in readiness for 2012.

Weymouth and Portland Harbour
Dorset will host the sailing, and the Weymouth and Portland harbour became the first completed 2012 venue on 28th November 2008. All sailing will be free for people to watch from any point along the shore.

Triumphs and challenges

HAMILTON STEERS TO VICTORY

Lewis Hamilton rocked Formula One motor-racing in November 2008 when he became its youngest ever World Champion. The 23-year-old had only been driving for the McLaren team for two seasons when he clinched the title at the Brazil Grand Prix. Interest in the sport soared and Lewis was on the front page of all the newspapers. Lewis started at a karting club as a young child and is now inspiring kids all over the country to follow in his tracks

The $20 million cricket game

The world's richest cricket game ever took place on 1st November 2008. Wealthy organiser Sir Allen Stanford challenged England to take on his team of 'superstars' on the island of Antigua in the Caribbean. The winning team were promised $20 million, with the losers earning nothing. Sadly, England were never in the running. Stanford captain Chris Gayle batted brilliantly, and his team went on to win with ease. Afterwards, the England skipper Kevin Pietersen said that the enormous payday on offer was just too distracting.

In the news

Sports Relief 2008

Top class athletes, celebrities and sporting legends all put on their trainers to support Sports Relief on Friday 14th March. A backbreaking host of challenges and donations raised a superb £28,523,047 for the charity. Highlights included: *Match of the Day* presenters Adrian Chiles and Alan Shearer cycling over 570 kilometres from Newcastle to London, and James Cracknell rowing, biking and swimming from the UK all the way to Africa.

Champion of champions

Test your sporting knowledge in this quick-fire results quiz!

1 Which golf team scored a surprise win in September 2008's Ryder Cup?
   a. USA
   b. Russia
   c. UK

2 Oxford won the 2008 Boat Race, but who was first past the post in 2009?
   a. Cambridge
   b. Oxford
   c. Durham

3 Who was Wimbledon's 2008 champion in the men's singles?
   a. Rafael Nadal
   b. Roger Federer
   c. Andy Murray

4 Who won the World Snooker Championship for the third time in April 2008?
   a. Stephen Hendry
   b. Ali Carter
   c. Ronnie O'Sullivan

5 Which rugby team claimed the Heineken Cup for the second time in three years?
   a. Munster
   b. Toulouse
   c. Wasps

Answers: 1a, 2b, 3a, 4c, 5a.

A tennis champ for Britain?

After reaching the quarter finals at Wimbledon, Andy Murray (pictured left) went on to have a dazzling year. The British tennis ace won two Masters events before losing out to David Nalbandian in the quarter finals of the Paris Masters in October 2008. In January 2009 he even beat tennis giants Roger Federer and Rafael Nadal in the Abu Dhabi World Tennis Championships.

Football crazy

SPAIN'S NIGHT OF GLORY

Euro 2008 was billed as one of the best football tournaments ever. National teams from Europe travelled to Austria in June 2008 to take part in 30 nail-biting games. Unfortunately England had been knocked out by Croatia earlier, with Northern Ireland also failing to reserve a place in the finals. Thousands gathered for the final in Vienna. It was destined to be Spain's night, with striker Fernando Torres scoring a 1-0 defeat in the 33rd minute.

Three cheers for the youngest player

Schoolboy Reuben Noble-Lazarus became the youngest ever player in the football league when he ran out for Barnsley on 30th September 2008.

The lad was only 15 years and 45 days old! He came on as a sub in a Tuesday evening Championship match against Ipswich Town. Because of his soccer skills, Reuben is allowed to miss school two days a week to attend training.

WE WON THE CUP!

In May 2008, Manchester United won the **Premier League** title for the 17th time. United thrashed Wigan 2-0 to end the season on 87 points, just two points above rivals Chelsea.

Portsmouth Manager Harry Redknapp scored his first **FA Cup** victory in May 2008. Pompey took on Cardiff City at Wembley Stadium, winning 1-0. Harry became the hero of Portsmouth, until he left to join Tottenham Hotspur in October 2008.

2008 **Carling Cup** winners Tottenham weren't able to repeat their success in 2009. Their Carling final against Manchester United was goalless after extra time, until the Red Devils got a 4-1 win on spot kicks.

Rangers reserved the **Scottish Cup** for themselves after beating Queen of the South 3-2 in the final at Hampden Park. The May 2008 victory hung in the balance until the 72nd minute, when Kris Boyd scored a header to take Rangers into the lead.

It was another glorious 3-2 score for Rangers in the **Scottish League Cup** final. Star striker Kris Boyd had a blinding match, scoring twice in normal time before clinching the match with a penalty kick. It was the 25th time that Rangers have won the League Cup.

It was the first ever all-English final when Manchester United battled Chelsea in the **Champions League**. Thousands travelled to Moscow's Luzhniki Stadium to see the sides draw 1-1. During the penalty shoot-out Chelsea captain John Terry missed the goal that would have seen his team became Champions of Europe. Instead United took the cup for an impressive third time.

Rangers fans were devastated when their team suffered defeat in the **Uefa Cup**. The Scots lost 2-0 against Russia's Zenit St Petersburg during a troubled night at the City of Manchester Stadium. Over 100,000 travelled to the city hoping to see the game.

Manchester United are crowned champions of the European Cup, in 2008.

Don't miss www.thefa.com, www.uefa.com and www.fifa.com for national, European and international results.

117

AVOIDING THE OBESITY TRAP

Most of us would think that it is adults and old people that need to worry about fitness, but a growing number of children and teens are found to be obese every year. Recent stats also show that three in ten boys and four in ten girls are not doing the minimum level of physical exercise recommended by the UK's Chief Medical Officer.

In the 2008 summer holidays the government released £3 million to address the problem of overweight kids, setting up special fitness camps. In August it was announced that mums and dads with obese youngsters might get into trouble for not looking after them properly. The government also started handing out free cookery books for 11-year-olds, full of healthy recipes.

The third UK Schools Games

Young athletes from all over the UK travelled to Bristol and Bath in 2008 for a special three day event. The occasion was the UK Schools Games – a huge competition for elite young sports people. Double gold swimming medallist Rebecca Adlington was there to welcome the 1,500 athletes that turned up to take part. Nine sports were on the programme, including judo, swimming, badminton and athletics.

Disappearing pitches

Kids today have less space to play sports, as more and more property developers buy up school fields. In 2009 however, new laws were introduced which hope to change all that. From now on English primary schools will have to get permission from the government before selling their land off to the highest bidder. Scotland and Wales also plan to do the same, although nothing is in place to protect pitches and fields in Northern Ireland.

Footie league tables banned

In September 2008, football bosses decided to change the rules for kids' under eights football. From now on all league tables have been banned for teams in this age group. The people in charge say that it's to stop children from worrying about winning, arguing that scoreboards put too much pressure on young players. Under eights are still free to play matches, but they won't be awarded cups or medals. Some parents argue that playing to win is important, but there already aren't any competitions for young kids in Wales and Northern Ireland. There are in Scotland, but no prizes are given out afterwards.

In March 2009 a new web film by the English Football Association also aimed to hush up pushy parents. The people running the game are concerned that mouthy mums and dads on the touchlines are turning their kids against soccer as well as reducing the number of people willing to train up as referees. Every year 7,000 refs turn their back on the beautiful game.

You could also stick or clip, newspaper cuttings or pictures that you'd like to keep.

Adam Fleming

1 **Describe your path into presenting Newsround?**
It was a very lucky break, really. I was studying at journalism school and I was helping out at the BBC on a training course for some news camera operators for a week. They filmed me doing some pretend news reports, which the boss of Newsround saw and thought: "Oooh – he might be a good presenter."

2 **Which of the past year's news stories particularly struck a chord with you?**
The recession. At first it sounded like a story about business and banks and companies, but now it seems to be affecting everyone. You can see it changing the way streets look – shops shutting down, lots of sales on, fewer people going out. It's very sad when you hear about people losing jobs and getting really stressed out about money. And the whole country seems to be talking about it all time.

3 **Was there anything you found difficult to cover and how do you cope with negative or distressing stories?**
The murder of the schoolboy Rhys Jones in Liverpool was a difficult story to cover. He got caught up in a fight between rival gangs that had nothing to do with him. You could see how upset his Mum and Dad were about it. Loads of people in Liverpool didn't want to talk to us because they were scared of the gangs. I always tell people that it's perfectly natural to be upset by sad news stories. The best way to deal with it is to talk about how you feel – bottling things up and pretending to be hard doesn't work.

4 **What do you do in a typical day?**
There isn't a typical day – that's why I love it! We start with a team meeting where we discuss who should cover what on Newsround that day. I join in via videophone from Manchester which is sometimes quite funny because people can get their wires crossed. Straight afterwards you get sent out to gather everything you need for your story. Then you put the pictures, script, interviews, music and graphics together. And THE most important thing? It's got to be ready by the time Newsround is on! Sometimes I'm out filming a report that will be shown on another day – then you have a bit more time and it's slightly less scary.

 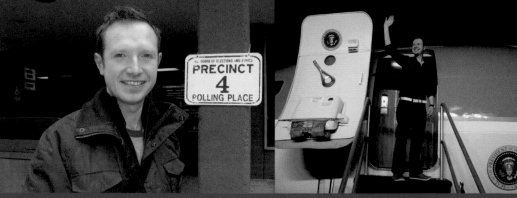

Adam in the USA for the American presidential election.

Adam out and about on the pre-election trail.

5 **What has been the biggest news story you've ever covered and what made it so important?**
The election of Barack Obama as President of the USA on November 4th 2008 was my highlight. I have a bit of a geeky interest in US politics and being there for the mega-historic moment when America elected its first black president was an experience I will never forget. I still get goosebumps when I think about how exciting it was on Election Night. And I've got amazing, happy memories of all the interesting people that I met in random places! I also got to see a rodeo in Phoenix, go trick-or-treating in Illinois, and eat the biggest pizza of my life in Chicago.

6 **Which major news story of this century would you most like to have covered?**
I covered the war in Iraq from the UK but never got the chance to report from the place itself. The war had a massive impact on so many countries around the world and will probably have an impact for the rest of the century. Some people think reporting in Iraq would be exciting – I think it would be interesting, sad and probably a bit scary.

7 **Who is the most interesting celebrity or public figure you've interviewed?**
My interview with Will Smith was the best nine minutes of my life! He is properly A-list but was very down-to-earth and even giggled at some of MY jokes. He made me laugh so much and made me feel like we had been friends for years. Although he hasn't been in touch since…

. . . and finally!

NUTTY NEWS

News stories can shock, sadden and please us, but sometimes a headline pops up that is so crazy it's hard to believe it's true! Telling fact from fiction on 1st April is even trickier. April Fool's 2008 and 2009 were full of daft tall stories, on a day when it's traditional to play pranks. Even Newsround got in on the act. The team ran a story launching a nationwide search to find performing cats for a new reality TV show called Kitten's Got Talent. The BBC iPlayer service caused a stir when it trailed a hoax nature programme about flying penguins. The clip featured a series called Miracles of Evolution showing life-like footage of Adelie penguins soaring over Antarctica, their little wings flapping in the sunshine. Several newspapers featured stories about the birds and David Attenborough was even interviewed about them on breakfast TV!

DAFT ART?

Artists are known for making sculptures that can confuse and outrage, but some exhibitions recently have taken the biscuit.

In October 2008 graffiti artist Banksy created a curious pet shop installation that got the art world talking. The animals inside the shop were models – a bizarre collection of pets doing even stranger things. Displays included a bowl full of swimming fish fingers and a rabbit wearing make-up! The exhibition looked wacky, but Banksy was trying to question how humans relate to the animals around us.

In January 2009, artist William Furlong displayed a baffling work of art in Bexhill, Sussex. The installation was a collection of 48 speakers hung on a wall, ea ch playing sounds from around the town. William said that the piece was trying to use noises instead of pictures to tell a story.

AMAZING NEWS STORIES

The top five stories that sounded like April Fool's tricks, but were actually true...

The year that arrived late
An extra second was added to clocks around the world at midnight on New Year's Eve 2008. Big Ben was adjusted and an extra pip was added to the BBC's countdown to the 1st January. The second was added to delay the start of the new year because the Earth is turning fractionally more slowly than it used to.

PE, but not as you know it
During 2008 and 2009 some schools decided to rethink their PE lessons. After complaints from pupils who can't stand exercising outside in the rain, teachers agreed to look at alternative indoor sports. New activities under review include yoga, cheerleading and martial arts.

The drum-playing gorilla
Fans of funny web clips spent hours in 2008 downloading footage of an ape playing the drums. The advert for Cadbury's Dairy Milk chocolate was the most requested silly internet search. In the clip the gorilla thrashes a kit to the beat of *In the Air Tonight* by Phil Collins.

Good times for Porsche
Top sportscar designers Porsche haven't been dented by the recession. In April 2008 the German manufacturers announced a four-fold rise in profits. Although Porsche sold less cars during the year, their stake in motor company Volkswagen kept the company's value high.

A £10 trip to space
No one could quite believe it when website www.voyage2space.com launched a competition to go and see the Earth from orbit. Players are required to pay £10 for the chance to win a place on the Virgin Galactic trip. The sub-orbital spaceflight is scheduled for 2010 and is worth over £107,000.

WEIRDEST OF THE YEAR?

On 22nd January 2009, a collection of people in wetsuits got ready to undertake the strangest ironing marathon ever! At least 128 divers jumped into a quarry in Gloucestershire in a bold bid to break an Australian world record. The divers managed to become the largest group of people to take part in an underwater ironing session! The attempt saw 86 divers successfully ironing within 10 minutes. As well as being a unique achievement, the weird event raised much-needed funds for the Royal National Lifeboat Institution.

to read the 'Most Popular Stories'.

Dealing with the news

If a story is affecting you or your life in a bad way, then there are things you can do to help you deal with the information you've heard and the way it is making you feel. Psychologist David Trickey answers your burning questions....

How do I know if what I'm feeling is normal?

'It's totally normal to have an emotional reaction to hearing a news story, whether that be feeling happy, sad, excited. But if the reaction is negative and prolonged then you might need help to deal with it. So if the feelings of sadness, anxiety or fear stay with you for a while, or make you not want to do things you normally do, then you might need help to cope or deal with your feelings.'

I'm having nightmares and wetting the bed....

'Sometimes people get physical reactions to things that have upset them. Some people find it difficult to sleep, have bad dreams, or start to wet the bed or have accidents during the day, or start to shake or breathe funny. If this is happening to you, you don't need to worry, but it probably isn't very nice for you, so it really would make sense to speak to someone about it so that they can help.'

What should I do to make myself feel better?

'Talking to someone is usually a good thing – especially if you are able to choose someone that you trust and that you know will listen carefully to you. Sometimes we find that just getting things out of our heads and into the space between us and someone else can be really helpful. This might be because it's better to have our feeling outside than in, or it might be that by talking it through we realise that things aren't quite as bad as we thought. Your parents, your teacher, your family, your friends, or your school counsellor if you have one, might be good people to speak to.'

Is there anything else I can do?

'Making sure that we still hang out with our friends is also really important. They could help us talk things through, but sometimes friends can help to distract us and make us think about other things. It might not be helpful to try to ignore the thing that is upsetting you, but sometimes it's helpful to not think about it all of the time.'

I keep seeing or hearing about the thing that upsets me...

'If something that has upset you is in the news a lot, then it can be difficult to avoid seeing it again, or we may even feel as if we want to watch it more. The trick is to find out enough about the story so that we don't need to watch anymore. Sometimes it's best to find out more by watching NR, and sometimes it's best to talk to someone else about it so that they can explain it in a helpful way.'

These words might help you understand some of the complicated themes and ideas that crop up in the news.

9/11
A series of attacks that took place across the USA on September 11th 2001. A group called Al-Quaeda hijacked two airliners and flew them into the Twin Towers of the World Trade Center in New York. A third plane was crashed near the Pentagon outside Washington DC and a fourth in Pennsylvania. Nearly 3,000 people died.

Cabinet
The most important ministers in the UK government. The members of the Cabinet meet with the Prime Minister at Downing Street once a week.

Carbon footprint
A way of measuring the impact our lives have on the environment. Our carbon footprint is a sign of how much fossil fuels we each burn up when we travel, heat our homes or consume electricity.

Climate change
A long-term and significant change in the Earth's weather patterns and temperatures that is out of the expected norm.

Counterfeit
Fake items made and sold as if they're authentic designer labels.

Custodial
A punishment for a crime that is served in prison.

Deploy
Move forces into position so that they can start military action.

Dictator
A person that governs a country or region without being voted into their post. Dictators make laws and hold absolute power over their regime.

Domestic violence
When somebody in the family is being violent at home. This may be adults hurting each other or one of them hurting the children.

DNA
A substance that is present in nearly all living organisms, carrying important genetic information about how they are made. DNA is inherited from parents.

Epicentre
The point on the surface of the Earth that sits directly above the origin of an earthquake.

Ethics
The moral principles that set down what we believe is good or bad behaviour.

Firewall
A barrier between your computer and the rest of the Internet, put in place to protect you as much as possible from viruses or hackers.

Flash flood
A sudden flood in one area that is caused by unusually high rainfall.

Greenhouse gas
Carbon dioxide and other gases that are thought to be contributing to climate change. The Earth is covered by layers of greenhouse gases that form a type of blanket that is just the right density to keep the temperature at safe levels.

Habitat
An animal's natural home.

House of Commons
The most powerful of Parliament's two houses. The Commons is the place where the politicians gather to discuss policies and make laws.

Independence
Being in charge of your own region or country, without any control from outside countries.

Obese
Being so overweight that it is bad for your health. Doctors work out if a person is obese by looking at how tall they are and how much they weigh.

Paparazzi
Self-employed photographers who persue celebrities to get photographs of them.

Primate
A type of intelligent mammal that includes monkeys, apes and humans.

Recession
A period of time when the economy is shrinking instead of growing. This is caused by a fall in the number of things that a country has made or sold.

Regenerate
Rebuild and redesign an area so that it becomes useful and important to the local community again.

Richter Scale
A method of measuring the size and power of an earthquake.

Trade union
An organisation made up of employees who have joined together to protect their rights, working conditions and pay.

UFO
An Unidentified Flying Object spotted in the sky that doesn't seem to have a reasonable scientific explanation.